Revelation
for Today

Images of Hope

RICHARD L. JESKE

FORTRESS PRESS   PHILADELPHIA

Library of Congress Cataloging in Publication Data

Jeske, Richard L., 1936–
   Revelation for today.

   Bibliography: p.
   1. Bible. N.T. Revelation—Commentaries.   I. Title.
BS2825.3.J47 1983   228'.07   82–16079
ISBN 0–8006–1693–6

9762H82   Printed in the United States of America   1–1693

*To my beloved
mother and father
Elsa Reisig Jeske
Walter Mendel Jeske
this book is
gratefully dedicated*

To you all angels, all the powers of heaven,
cherubim and seraphim, sing in endless praise:
  Holy, holy, holy Lord,
  God of power and might,
  heaven and earth are full of your glory.
The glorious company of apostles praise you.
The noble fellowship of prophets praise you.
The white-robed army of martyrs praise you.
                —From the *Te Deum Laudamus*

Contents

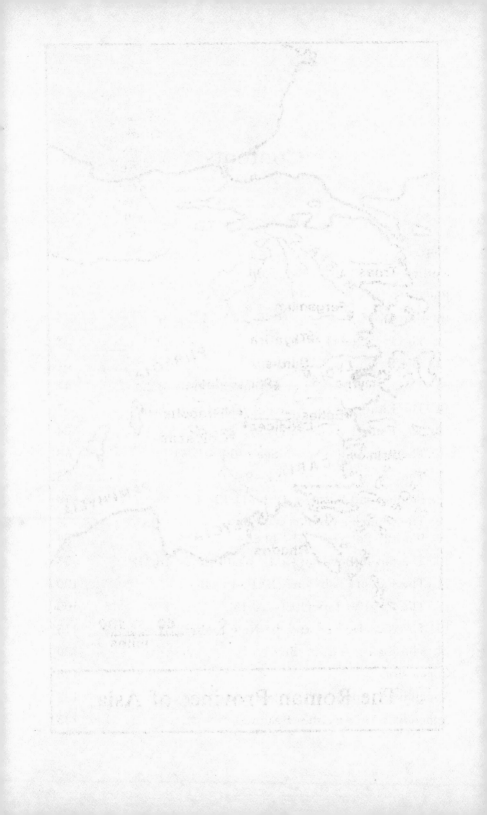

Troas

MYSIA

Pergamum

Thyatira

LYDIA
Sardis

Smyrna
Philadelphia

PHRYGIA

Ephesus
Hierapolis
Laodicea
Colossae

(Patmos)

CARIA

AEGEAN SEA

LYCIA

PAMPHYLIA

Rhodes

0   50   100
miles

The Roman Province of Asia

Outline of the
Book of Revelation

Preface

In sports "The Four Horsemen" is the nickname once given to a talented football backfield coached by the legendary Knute Rockne of Notre Dame. In politics the "One Thousand Year Reign" that Adolf Hitler had promised for Germany came to its end in 1945. In literature *Armageddon* is the title of a novel by Leon Uris about post–World War II Germany through the time of the Berlin Airlift. In film *The Seventh Seal* is the title of a motion picture by Ingmar Bergman on the subject of human mortality, and *Apocalypse Now* is the name given to another film directed by Francis Ford Coppola on the subject of the Vietnam War. All these titles have their origin in the symbolism of the Book of Revelation, the last book in the Christian Bible.

Hardly a Christmas or Easter season passes without the opportunity for us to hear the music of Handel's *Messiah*. The most popular segment of this oratorio is the "Hallelujah" chorus, with the majestic words:

Hallelujah! for the Lord God omnipotent reigneth.
The kingdom of this world is become the kingdom of our Lord, and of His Christ; and He shall reign for ever and ever.
King of Kings, and Lord of Lords. Hallelujah!

These words are taken from the Book of Revelation (see 19:6, 11:15, 19:16), as are the words of the final chorus (5:12–13):

Worthy is the Lamb that was slain, and hath redeemed us to God by His blood, to receive power, and riches, and wisdom, and strength, and honor, and glory, and blessing.
Blessing and honor, glory and power, be unto Him that sitteth upon the throne, and unto the Lamb, for ever and ever.

1

Liturgies now in use in American churches employ the imagery of the Book of Revelation as effective vehicles for congregational worship. In each of the Communion Liturgies in the *Lutheran Book of Worship,* in one form or another, are the words of the Hymn of Praise:

> Worthy is Christ, the Lamb who was slain,
> whose blood set us free to be people of God.
> Power and riches and wisdom and strength,
> and honor and blessing and glory are his.
> This is the feast of victory for our God.
> Alleluia.

In the revised *Book of Common Prayer* now in use in The Episcopal Church the imagery of the worship scenes in the Book of Revelation is clearly recalled in one of the eucharistic prayers:

And therefore we praise you, joining with the heavenly chorus, with prophets, apostles, and martyrs, and with all those in every generation who have looked to you in hope, to proclaim with them your glory, in their unending hymn. . . .

In both of these congregational worship books the ancient *maranatha* "Come, Lord Jesus!" used at the conclusion of the Book of Revelation, is one of the congregational responses in the eucharistic Liturgy.

The wealth of liturgical material within the Book of Revelation itself already reflects the worship practice of the ancient Christian churches: hymns (4:11), salutations (1:4), thanksgivings (11:17), liturgical gestures (1:17), blessings (1:3), and benedictions (22:21), including its own version of the *Sanctus:*

> Holy, holy, holy, is the Lord God Almighty,
> who was and is and is to come! (4:8)

But for all the wealth of liturgical material found in the Book of Revelation, it is not as a worship resource that this writing is generally known. Instead, its symbolic imagery and its orientation toward the future have made it the most mysterious book in the New Testament—perhaps even the most misunderstood and misinterpreted book in the Bible. The assumption that the Book of Revelation, with its cryptic portraiture, must be speaking

about world events as they unravel before our very eyes has led
to the wildest and most misleading speculation, causing needless
anxiety and little real appreciation for the intentions of the ancient author.

For instance, a little tract has circulated recently which con-
tends that the Universal Product Code marks on grocery items
used in rapid-price scanning systems are foretold in Rev. 13:17:
" . . . no one can buy or sell unless he has the mark, that is, the
name of the beast or the number of its name." In other words,
such marking systems are, according to the anonymous author of
this tract, only an example of the growing and pervasive influence
of the "beast," namely Satan, in the world today.

The most popular of the apocalyptic entrepreneurs is Hal
Lindsey, the author of the sensationalist book *The Late Great
Planet Earth*, whose combination of fundamentalist biblical interpretation and outright scare tactics have resulted in gaining
him an extremely wide readership. His predictions have needed
readjustment in the light of deadlines which have come and gone
without fulfillment. But undaunted, Mr. Lindsey himself was featured in a television commercial advertising his new recording
which asks whether the beast of Revelation 13 is actually the
United States. Buy the record ($13.95) and see!

But according to the February/March 1980 "special report to
members of The 700 Club," entitled "Pat Robertson's Perspective," the beast of Revelation 13 is actually the Soviet Union,
which is presently about to attack Israel "to gain unrestricted
access to Middle East oil plus a land bridge to the mineral wealth
of Africa." The economy of Western Europe will be doomed and
the world will see the rise of a "counterfeit Messiah," a satanic
figure "more malevolent than Adolph Hitler," who in 1980 was
"approximately twenty-seven years old" and was being groomed
for his sinister task. His nightmarish seven-year reign is the time
of the "Great Tribulation," which will come to an end with the
return of Christ, who will destroy the Antichrist at the battle of
Armageddon (see Rev. 16:16). "Then Christ will lift his saints
both dead and living to be with him (the 'Rapture') and he will
lift Israel to a preeminent role among the nations of the earth."

Such speculation, which purports to unravel the "real meaning" of the Book of Revelation, is not new. Throughout the history of the church interpreters have sought to explain this writing allegorically, spiritualistically, and mystically, attempting in some way to relate the words of the ancient author to events of every new period in history. In the time following the Reformation the interpretation of Revelation was applied to the sixteenth- and seventeenth-century struggles within the church, with both Protestants and Catholics applying the text dogmatically and polemically against their respective opponents. The work of the respected pietistic interpreter Johann Albrecht Bengel (1687–1752), which influenced interpretation into the nineteenth century, identified the pope as the beast of Revelation 13 and determined June 18, 1836 as the beginning of the millennium. A Roman Catholic interpreter writing in 1785 under the pseudonym "Pastorini" identified Luther as the fallen star of Revelation 9 and Mohammed as the beast of Revelation 13. As late as the mid-nineteenth century one German scholar (Hengstenberg) saw the millennium as having already come to its end with the passing of the old German Empire, and he equated the rise of Gog and Magog (Revelation 20) with the 1848 revolution.

For the past hundred years serious exegetical work on the Book of Revelation has moved away from previous efforts to equate elements in the writing to current historical events. Instead, research has concentrated on the relationship of Revelation to its own time, to other examples of its own type of literature as it existed in antiquity, and to the literary and theological traditions employed by the author. Much has been gained from such recent research in terms of our knowledge of the author, his own historical situation, and his basic intentions, knowledge which now can inform our assessment of his writing and bring us to a more positive appreciation of it.

Nevertheless, especially as this century draws to a close, we shall be hearing more and more modern-day apocalyptists imposing their own agendas on the Book of Revelation. What would be an appropriate response? One option, of course, is to write off both the book and its interpreters as a lost cause. Why get involved in useless argumentation and groundless speculation? That may in fact be the easiest way to go. But thoughtful students of the New Testament will not be satisfied with that option. Since the Book of Revelation is in the New Testament it deserves to be studied, understood as best as is possible, and appreciated for what it is and for what it offers to us. But all this must be done on its own terms rather than on ours so that we do not make of it something that its author did not intend for it to be.

In our present study, then, we shall be asking about the message of the Book of Revelation, beginning first of all with a brief summary of past methods of interpretation and moving on to questions about the author and his readers. We shall ask such questions in order to inform our own approach to this writing. For instance, who was the author and what were his main intentions? Was he attempting to frighten his audience or to bring them a word of encouragement and hope? Was the symbolic imagery meaningful to his original readers or did they have to wait twenty centuries before its meaning could be discovered? How does the situation shared by the author and his original audience shed light on the symbolism in the book? What kind of a writing is an "apocalypse"? Such historical questions, necessary as they are, nevertheless will remain a prelude to our hearing the message John of Patmos wishes his readers to hear, namely, the prophetic good news of God's presence among us.

This book grew out of a study series published during 1981 in *The Lutheran*, the magazine of the Lutheran Church in America. The author was able to expand the series into book form during a sabbatical study leave granted by the Lutheran Theological Seminary at Philadelphia. This study leave was generously supported by the reception of the Franklin Clark Fry Fellowship Award granted by Aid Association for Lutherans, and also by a Seminary Sabbatical Fellowship awarded by Lutheran Brotherhood. To these institutions the author expresses his deepest gratitude.

Many others contributed to this project. First of all, the editors and readers of the study series provided many helpful comments and criticisms, as did also a close community of colleagues also on sabbatical in Tübingen. But there was also the joyful sharing of a family community, expressed by the loving question, "Dad, how can we help?" So the map on page vii was contributed by my son Mark, ten years of age, and the arrangement of the *RSV* text at the beginning of each chapter was done by my daughter Nancy, twelve years of age. The painstaking duty of proofreading and correcting the manuscript was done by my wife Emily. This book, then, is accompanied by the gratitude of a husband and a father—and also that of a son, for the encouragement and support over the decades shown by his own parents, to whom this book is dedicated.

Tübingen, Germany
February 23, 1982
The Day of Polycarp, Bishop of Smyrna, Martyr
Bartholomaeus Ziegenbalg, Witness

Introduction

No other book of the Bible has attracted so much attention and caused so much consternation as the Book of Revelation. No other book has been so widely read and so wildly misread. There are many people who find it difficult to get its name straight: its name is not "Revelations" but "Revelation." The name comes from the opening line of the book, where it stands in the singular. For all the attention given to it, the Book of Revelation remains incomprehensible for many people, and many others have simply given up on it. Yet it is a common experience among parish pastors that when the time comes for the new Bible class to choose which biblical book to study next, Revelation always finishes strongly in the voting.

For many people there is only one way to interpret the Book of Revelation, namely, as a book of "prophecy," and they understand the word "prophecy" to mean a prediction of future events. It is then natural to view the book as containing a series of predictions about the future, a book of "revelations" (and thus the misnomer) about events yet to come in world history. It comes as a surprise to such people that there are other ways to interpret Revelation and that various methods have already long been practiced, including their own, for centuries in fact. From such past attempts there is much to be learned, not the least of which is some caution about the approach we should use today.

Methods of Interpretation, Past and Present

The use of Revelation as predictive of events at the end of world history reaches back to the earliest stages of Christian biblical interpretation. Justin Martyr (ca. 100–165) is the earliest of the church fathers to comment on Revelation, alluding to it only

once in his writings. In Rev. 20:1–8 Justin found support for the
doctrine of the millennium, the reign of Christ on earth for one
thousand years, a doctrine which Justin said all orthodox Christians believed. The practice of developing doctrines by combining references from various books of the Bible was done also in
the early church. The church father Irenaeus (ca. 130–200) wrote
that since God created the world in six days and rested on the
seventh, and since one day with the Lord is as one thousand
years, the world would last six thousand years, after which would
begin the one-thousand-year reign of Christ, a period of rest and
blessing.

This method of combining biblical texts produced the doctri-
nal tradition of the Antichrist, the dreaded figure who would
appear at the end of world history. This tradition, begun perhaps
even before Irenaeus, was based on a combination of passages
from Daniel 2 and 7, 1 John 2:22, 2 John 7, and Revelation 13 and
17. It should be noted that the word "Antichrist" does not occur
in the Book of Revelation, yet even modern-day interpreters continue to use the term in connection with the images in the book.
Happily, we have come to know that combining "proof texts" to
support doctrines unimagined by the individual authors themselves is not the best way to approach the Scriptures.

In the fourth century Christianity attained the status of the
official religion of the Roman Empire, a situation quite different
from that experienced by the original readers of the Book of
Revelation. The popular interpretation of Christ's one-thousand-year reign was that it was now in progress: the church was
now enjoying the benefits of Christ's rule, which had begun with
his birth in Bethlehem. That meant that as the year 1000 approached anxieties heightened, for Satan was then to be loosed
(cf. Rev. 20:3), and the hour of Antichrist would be at hand.
People donated their property and wealth to the church, religious revivals sprang up everywhere, and the church's worship
services were filled. But the tenth century came and went, and
the schedule for the millennium suddenly needed readjustment.

The focus of interpretation after the tenth century began to
shift, for with the establishment of the church as the official state
religion, the symbolism in Revelation which depicted a repres-

sive secular government opposed to Christianity lost its force. The church itself became increasingly powerful and soon asserted its own superiority over the state even in secular affairs: kings and emperors could assume their rule only with the approval of the pope of Rome. A materialistic and secularistic papacy now became the foil for popular interpretations of the Book of Revelation.

For example, the influential monk Joachim of Flora (1132–1202) applied Revelation's symbols to religious-historical developments: the beast of Revelation 13 is Islam, whose death wound was being inflicted by the Crusades. "Babylon" (Rev. 17:5ff.) is the Holy Roman Empire now sunk in secularism and vice. With the demise of this empire the church would be renewed and a new monastic order (or two) would emerge which would promote the devotional and contemplative life throughout the world. This latter prediction was seen to be fulfilled in the rise of the Franciscan and Dominican orders shortly after Joachim's death.

Joachim's students continued his method of religious-historical interpretation but pursued a much more openly antipapal course than had their teacher. The struggle of the papacy for secular power reached its high point with Pope Innocent III's proclamation in 1198: "I am the vicar of Jesus Christ, the successor of Peter, and I am placed between God and man, less than God, but greater than man: I judge all men, but by no man am I to be judged." Such bold and exclusive claims for secular power along with the materialism and corruption displayed in the church brought heavy criticism from the new contemplative orders, and soon the papacy was declared to be the Antichrist and the beast symbols of Revelation 13 were applied to specific popes. The various major reform movements from the thirteenth through the fifteenth centuries—the Waldenses in France, the followers of Jan Huss in Bohemia and of John Wycliffe in England—all were agreed that the papacy was the Antichrist and that the Book of Revelation was to be directed against the Roman Catholic Church.

Martin Luther was therefore not at all the first to refer to the papacy as the Antichrist. Interpretation had moved in that direc-

tion for three centuries before him, employing the traditional
fourfold method of investigating the text, a method which
reached back to the third century. This fourfold method taught
the interpreter to seek a literal, an allegorical, a moral, and a
mystical meaning in each scriptural item. Luther himself had
employed these methods in his own exegetical lectures but
eventually came to mistrust them because of the subjectivity
they encouraged on the part of the interpreter. What we should
hear when we read the Bible is the Word of *God*, a Word not
dependent on official church authorities for its meaning nor dependent on the individualistic interpretations demanded by
spiritualistic enthusiasts.

In the year 1522 Luther wrote a preface to the Book of Revelation for inclusion in his German translation of the New Testament. In this preface he complained about the book's lack of
clarity and said that because the author had not spoken clearly
about Christ and the gospel, as apostles should, the book could
be considered neither apostolic nor prophetic. Referring to Rev.
22:7 Luther wrote: "They are supposed to be blessed who keep
what is written in this book; and yet no one knows what that is, to
say nothing of keeping it. This is just the same as if we did not
have the book at all. And there are many far better books available for us to keep." In this preface Luther chose not to give a
general interpretation of the book and stressed that his opinions
about it should not hinder others from developing their own.

In 1530, however, Luther wrote a second preface to Revelation, noting that many attempts to interpret the book had
achieved no certainty about its meaning. "Some have even
brewed it into many stupid things out of their own heads," he
said. Then almost as if he felt pushed into doing so he offered his
own summary interpretation of the book, basing it on the traditional method of religious-historical interpretation, relating
John's images to the struggles against heretical teachings which
had plagued the Christian church throughout its history. He too
had come to see the Roman church as a "counterfeit church of
external holiness," and his interpretation of Revelation, by his
own admission, pursued an antipapal course. This course may
have been prompted by his desire to see the work on the Augs-

burg Confession in 1530 take a more strongly antipapal direction. Regarding the beast of Revelation 13 he noted that the second beast had to be the pope, who had "restored the fallen Roman Empire and conveyed it from the Greeks to the Germans," as reflected in one of the beast's heads that was mortally wounded and healed again (Rev. 13:3, 12). (For Luther's prefaces see the American edition of *Luther's Works*, vol. 35.)

Luther's ideas about Revelation may strike us as odd, even somewhat embarrassing to Protestant Christians of today. Yet Luther's interpretation must be seen within the context of the religious-historical method used by a series of reform movements in the late Middle Ages. Furthermore, Luther paved the way for an interpretation of Revelation which, apart from its detailed application to his own time, can still be helpful today. First of all, he saw its major message to be one of promise and hope, namely, that the people of God will not be overcome by oppression and persecution, tribulation and suffering. Second, Luther drew out the political and social implications of the book's message, namely, the ultimate failure of any human institution, be it political or ecclesiastical, which attempts to assume the place of God among human beings and to set itself over the Word of the gospel.

Protestant scholarship after Luther continued to lob its exegetical missiles at the Roman Catholic Church, and Catholic authors lobbed them back in return. Throughout the sixteenth and seventeenth centuries, even into the eighteenth, one side saw the other as a new embodiment of the forces of evil described in Revelation. On the one side it was suggested that the angel from heaven with the everlasting gospel in Rev. 14:6 should be seen as Martin Luther himself, while on the other side the eventual triumph of the forces of good in Revelation should be seen as a prediction of the eventual triumph of the Roman Catholic Church.

During the seventeenth century various scholars suggested a so-called recapitulation theory of interpretation. This theory held that Revelation should not be seen as foretelling the future events of world history in a linear sequence, that is, one after another until the end of time. Rather, the various series of visions—seven seals, seven trumpets, seven bowls—were each different pictures of the same eschatological drama. The letters to the seven churches represented seven stages of church history in which the eschatological drama would repeat itself anew in each stage. This "recapitulation" theory is still alive today among those who wish to use Revelation as a book of predictions about present and future events, often with the loosely applied argument that "history repeats itself."

It was not until the nineteenth century that scholarship began to seek the relationship of the Book of Revelation to its own time. In 1870 a scholar by the name of Karl Immanuel Nitzsch coined the term "apocalyptic" to refer to a number of biblical and non-biblical writings which contained characteristics similar to those found in Revelation. Such writings included the Old Testament books of Ezekiel and Daniel, the apocryphal book 4 Ezra, and the noncanonical writing called Ethiopic Enoch written between 100 B.C. and A.D. 100. In 1832 a commentary written by Friedrich Luecke applied Nitzsch's suggestion to view Revelation within a distinct literary context and asked what the original author's symbols were to mean to readers of his own day. For the last one hundred fifty years since Luecke, then, serious scholarship on Revelation has concentrated on the question of the original situation of the writer and his audience, what his symbols and imagery originally meant to them, what traditions he might have shared with them, and what literary sources he might have employed as he wrote.

This does not at all mean that we can no longer apply the message of Revelation to our day. Quite the contrary, we are better able to apply its message to our own time when we have first seen how that message originally related to its own time. We are also able to provide some helpful controls to modern-day interpretation rather than to allow utter subjectivity to run rampant with the text, with every new author using Revelation as a foil for his or her own personal likes or dislikes.

So we shall approach the book with the understanding that it had something to say to its original hearers and readers. We shall ask about the author's situation, his intentions and goals in writing the book, and we shall ask how his message relates to this

context, the Christian church in the Roman Empire at the end of
the first century A.D. When we have seen it as a means of communication between its original author and audience, we shall
then be able more appropriately to see how it communicates to
us today.

What Is an Apocalypse?

The Book of Revelation is the only complete apocalypse in the
New Testament. Other apocalyptic material is to be found in the
New Testament, but only piecemeal—for example, Mark 13 (and
parallels in Matthew 24 and Luke 21), 1 Thess. 4:13–17, 1 Cor.
15:20–28, 2 Thess. 2:3–14, 1 John 2:18, 2 Pet. 2:1—3:13, 1 Tim.
4:1, and 2 Tim. 3:1–9. The letter of Jude is almost fully apocalyptic in content, but it presents itself as a letter, while the Book of
Revelation expressly calls itself an apocalypse, "the revelation
(apocalypse) of Jesus Christ" (1:1).

In the Old Testament the Book of Daniel is referred to as an
"apocalypse" even though it lacks that self-designation and even
though its final six chapters more properly fit that designation
than do the first six. There are apocalyptic sections in the prophetic books of Isaiah (24—27) and Zechariah (9—14), sections
which may have been added to these books by later editors. The
apocryphal book of 4 Ezra, and the noncanonical books of
Ethiopic Enoch (or 1 Enoch) and 2 Baruch, writings which appeared between 100 B.C. and A.D. 100, are also to be included in
the study of apocalyptic literature (see Appendix A, pp. 132–
34). Various writings among the Dead Sea Scrolls are catego-
rized by some scholars as apocalyptic, and a number of Christian
apocalypses appeared after A.D. 100.

The word "apocalypse" is a Greek word meaning "revelation"
or "unveiling." In biblical research the word is generally used
for a writing whose stated purpose is to reveal or unveil the
secrets of the future which God has in store for humanity. The
strict categorizing of apocalyptic literature is somewhat ham-
pered by the fact that not all characteristics which commonly
occur in these writings always occur in each one. But that in itself
should be considered a characteristic of apocalyptic literature: a
general sharing of topics, ideas, and linguistic style without a

strict uniformity in structure or content. One cannot speak of an
"apocalyptic movement" if by that one means a dogmatically
fixed theological or sociological phenomenon.

It is very difficult to speak precisely about the origins of
apocalypticism. The Old Testament materials suggest a theological confrontation with the traditional notion that the events of
world history were the results of God's action, whether of his
favor or his judgment. A time in Israel's history which provided a
context for such a theological confrontation would be in the af-
termath of the Babylonian destruction of Jerusalem in 586 B.C.
The loss of Israel's kingship, temple, and land resulted in a growing pessimism toward the political-historical realm as the arena
of God's activity. Had not the events borne out the fact that the
forces of evil were at work within these events? Therefore also
the restoration of the people to the land under Cyrus in 539 B.C.
and the rebuilding of the Temple were suspect: the political and
religious leadership had worked out their compromises under
alliance with the Persians. Such pessimism about present historical events led to a concentration on the future when God would
intervene to establish his new world order.

Many of the features generally found in apocalyptic writings
can be explained as arising out of this early pessimism about
present political and historical phenomena. The means of expression employed by apocalyptic writers were derived from a
common cultural heritage which included ancient national and
international mythological imagery. Certainly one vehicle for the
expression of this pessimism is the ancient story, found in both
Hebrew and Babylonian literature, of the primeval struggle between the forces of chaos and creation. The creation is the result
of the victory over the forces of chaos, but for the apocalyptic
writers the struggle is on once again as the chaos-forces have
entered the present historical scene and co-opted its institutions
for their own evil designs.

For the apocalyptic writers, then, the end can come only as a
decisive interruption of world-historical events, often portrayed
on a cosmic scale, when God will destroy the present political
and social structures and restore his people as part of his new
creation. When this will occur can become the object of a given

apocalyptist's speculation, sometimes based on astrological reckoning, but more often based on a periodization of history into time segments whose length is already predetermined by God. The outcome of the struggle is never in doubt, yet present conditions indicate how fiercely the evil forces are at work. Therefore dualistic terminology becomes an important vehicle for apocalyptic descriptions of the present struggle: the forces of good over against the forces of evil, God and his angelic hosts over against Satan and his angels; the righteous are contrasted with the godless, and the present evil age with the glory of the age to come. In this literature we shall often see the human being depicted as weak, caught in the evil web of the forces of darkness, who may be redeemed only by God's victory, which will include the resurrection of the martyrs to live eternally with all the saints. Often God's victory is seen to be the accomplishment of his "Sent One," his servant, understood either as an individual or as a corporate symbol for the whole community of God's people.

Virtually all of these elements mentioned here from the larger context of traditional apocalyptic literature are reflected in the Book of Revelation. It is important, though, to notice the subtle divergences from that general tradition which are also found in Revelation. Every divergence can in itself be a theological statement which the author wishes his readers to hear. For example, the author wishes to view God's future as a transformation of this world rather than a destruction of it. The world is God's creation and the people in it are always the object of God's invitation, to the very last point in the struggle and even beyond it (cf. Rev. 18:4; 22:2). Thus the author intends to promote mutual responsibility among people in this world (rather than a contemptuous death wish toward others in this world) and encouragement and consolation in the present rather than fear in view of an imminent conflagration. This stands in contrast to modern-day apocalyptic writers and movements that build their followings by promoting anxiety about the future and contempt toward the rest of the world, especially toward those who do not think as they do.

The author chooses the word "apocalypse" (revelation) to introduce his writing (1:1). It would seem more appropriate therefore to refer to this writing as "the Apocalypse" or even "the Revelation," designations various modern authors have chosen to use. The present writer, however, will continue to refer to the book simply as "Revelation" mainly because that is the designation popularly used today. But the choice of the word "apocalypse" is the way the author of Revelation suggests comparisons with a distinct literary tradition with which he sets himself in dialogue.

The Language and Structure of Revelation

By choosing to write an "apocalypse" the author is making a conscious decision to address certain areas of concern in terms of a distinct literary style. Apocalyptic literature has its own topics and its own manner of approaching these topics. In the previous section we discussed some of the topics commonly found in apocalypticism; now we should explore the manner in which these topics are approached.

First, in every apocalypse the revelation is mediated to the human recipient by a heavenly being. In the case of Daniel it is the angel Gabriel (8:16); in the case of Revelation it is an angelic messenger sent from Christ (1:1). In this way the apocalyptic writer wishes to state that the message he now passes on is a message he has first received. It is not his own. This is quite compatible with the Christian understanding of the word "prophecy," which the author of Revelation also uses to describe his work (1:3) and which we shall discuss shortly. The revelation usually comes in the form of visions, often followed by an auditory element, usually an interpretive comment or a further instruction from the heavenly messenger. In Revelation, seeing and hearing are closely related, as we shall also discuss shortly.

The use of symbolic imagery is also a sign of reception. It is often overlooked that the employment of symbolism is a thoroughly communal feature, for the author's choice of symbols is determined by the community for which the writing is intended. In the case of Revelation, some of the symbols may represent code language already in use in the community, while others may represent material used in the community's worship. Still other symbolic imagery may represent older apocalyptic material circulating in the author's community which the author now uses in the service of his own message. Such symbols evidently had meaning for the author's original audience and therefore indicate the communal nature of the writing. We learn more about the symbols by learning more about the audience and its liturgical and literary traditions.

If the author of Revelation is in touch with his readers' liturgical and literary traditions, he is also in touch with their history. And we learn from the outset that he is himself involved in that history (1:9): his readers are experiencing persecution, poverty (2:9), and execution (2:13). He now speaks to them as one of them, for he sees in the present circumstances not simply darkness but challenge and hope. He draws upon the resources available to them in their common life and faith, resources which include the Scriptures of the Old Testament as well as material in use in the devotional life of the churches. The particular congregations he addresses, at least some of them, have also experienced the ministry of the apostle Paul and very likely have had access to his writings. Various similarities in theological content and terminology between Revelation and the letters of Paul will be pointed out in the chapters which follow. The language used in Revelation was by no means new to these churches but reflected the traditions which were very much alive in their community fellowship. John of Patmos draws upon these living traditions in order to offer images of hope in a time of oppression.

The careful use of imagery is paralleled by the deliberate structure that the author gives to this writing, as a glance at the outline provided at the beginning of this book will indicate. The initial chapter describes the prophet's call. Then we have the letters to the seven churches (2:1—3:22), which provide rather detailed descriptions of the audience. The next section (4:1—22:5) contains a series of seven vision-cycles, prefaced by the author's portrayal of the heavenly court (4:1—5:14) and followed by the vision of God's new city (21:5—22:5). This entire section (4:1—22:5) is, of course, the most difficult to outline, with some commentators seeing seven vision-cycles and others only four. We do not wish to be dogmatic in suggesting the outline we find most applicable, and we recognize that any outline offered after

the fact will tend to be somewhat arbitrary. However, outlines
are of some use in attempting to relate the various sections of the
book to the whole as well as to each other. It is for that purpose
that we have offered an outline at the beginning of this book.

One of the author's techniques is to interlock some of the
vision-cycles, a technique which provides difficulties for those
who wish to view his material in a historically linear fashion. For
instance, the opening of the seventh seal actually sets in motion
the next cycle, that of the seven trumpets (8:1ff.); the seventh
trumpet inaugurates the next cycle, the visions of conflict
(11:15ff.); and one of the angels of the seven-bowls vision shows
John the visions of Babylon's fall (17:1ff.). Furthermore, there is
some close parallelism between various cycles, especially between the visions of the seven trumpets and the seven bowls, as a
comparison of the ingredients will show: the second element has
to do with the sea, the third the rivers, the fifth the nether world,
and the sixth mentions the river Euphrates (cf. 8:8—9:25 with
16:3–14). Similar ingredients are also found in the sections
14:1–20 and 19:1–16.

By structuring his writing in this way, the author does not wish
to invite a linear-temporal interpretation of his symbols. The
message that he wants all his readers to hear is that Christ
crucified is the victor whose own victory offers promise, hope,
and therefore a future to God's people. This one message is portrayed by various word pictures, and those who use the word
pictures to chart the sequence of future world historical events
have missed the significance of the interconnectedness of the
imagery which the author has achieved by his technique of interlocking vision-cycles. Accordingly, we are able to see the entire
section of the interlocking vision-cycles under the heading "The
Prophetic Vision" rather than "The Prophetic Visions" in order
to emphasize the interconnectedness of the imagery in the service of the author's one message.

The question of what the apocalyptic writer consciously is
both allowing and demanding of his readers when he chooses to
write in apocalyptic style is interesting. What is his audience
invited to do when they read or hear his word pictures? My
friend Richard Hopkins, the surrealist artist, takes great joy in
inviting his audience to respond to a new painting. But when we

ask him if what we see there is actually intended by him, he refuses to answer. He does not wish to limit the interpreter to his original conceptions. More than that, he does not wish to limit the *meaning of the painting.* However, we are uncomfortable with that. Does his refusal to provide controls for our interpretation suggest that *any* interpretation is legitimate? Not at all, for the interpretation already is limited by both the author's and the interpreter's own places in time and space. Thoughtful interpretation will always begin with the history and influences at work on the artist and then will be honest enough to recognize the possibilities and limitations imposed by the history and influences at work on the interpreter as well. Within the work of art, there already exist certain controls imposed by culture and tradition: the color brown will generally not be used for a bridal gown, nor will a downward arc generally suggest great elation. A given interpretation can also say as much, if not more, about the interpreter than it does about the artist.

The use of symbol both allows and requires the audience to interact with the artist or author. On the other hand, some interaction has already taken place if the artist or author creates a work with a particular audience in mind. In the process of creating the work the artist or author chooses the symbols which are able to convey meaning to a particular audience. Such symbols are shared by artist and audience from within the heritage of a common historical and cultural context. But because they are *symbols,* the possibility exists for proper interpretation outside that common historical and cultural context.

The author of Revelation indicates that his immediate audience is "the seven churches that are in Asia" (1:4). Therefore the language and symbolic imagery that he chooses, in order to appeal to their understanding, is drawn from the historical and cultural context he shares with them. His choice of the number *seven,* however, the number in his culture for completeness, means that he envisions an audience not limited only to the churches he specifically names. His work projects itself beyond its immediate context to the entire Christian church. It invites Christians of every time and place to interpret it for themselves. It allows and demands their interaction.

Because the author's symbols have actual points of reference within the history and culture of his hearers, thoughtful interpretation will begin with that original context. But the symbolism in Revelation—and this is what causes so much fascination with the book—is not static, sedimented symbolism, with each symbol fixed forever on only one point of reference. The symbols in Revelation have a "tensive" quality, that is, their meaning is not exhausted by any one referent. The symbols invite many comparisons: a symbol may be *like* a given referent *but not equal* to it. For example, the beast of Chapter 13 is a symbol for the Roman Empire; however, the empire in itself is symbolic of any human institution which sets itself over God in this world. Appropriate interpretation, then, will avoid limiting this symbol to any one point of historical reference and will retain the dynamic quality that a *symbol* in fact allows.

There is one set of symbols in Revelation which has only a single, fixed reference point, namely, the christological symbols. These symbols will allow no other reference point than Christ crucified as the victor whose own victory guarantees the future for God's people. There are a number of richly drawn images which clearly refer to Christ alone. In this case, because of the nature of this one central subject, the reference point cannot fully be described by any one symbol. In fact, the entire complex of Revelation's symbolic imagery has its creative ground in the cross of the Christ who now lives. And it is this reference point from which any new interaction with John's word pictures must move.

Therefore a good rule of thumb to use when evaluating modern interpretations of the Book of Revelation is to ask where the emphasis of interpretation has been placed. Has the interpreter concentrated only on the meaning he or she perceives behind each individual symbol, or has that interpreter related the symbols to the central message which pervades the book, to the good news of the crucified one who now lives? Has the interpreter invited the reader to coordinate further application of the symbols to this central message? John of Patmos intended to bring a word of encouragement and hope to his audience, and therefore his message centered on the victory of the crucified Christ, the one who died and is alive for evermore (1:18; 2:8). Any use of

John's writing to frighten people and to increase their anxieties by means of speculative predictions supposedly based on John's symbols, as some interpreters recently have done, is an inappropriate use of John's writing. The good news of the one who died and is now alive offers hope, not anxiety, to God's people. It means that God's future is their future, and that through the most tragic of circumstances God's offer of life is still good.

The Author of Revelation and His Readers

In most of the popular attempts to unravel the secrets of the Book of Revelation, the original author and the situation of his readers are largely forgotten. As modern sensation-seeking interpreters strive to gain attention by applying the ingredients of Revelation to current events, they seem to ignore the fact that the original author had a message to give to his original audience. Certainly we should not want to say that the original readers would have to wait twenty centuries before they could understand what their leader wrote to them in their time.

We have learned that the Scriptures are best understood when the attempt is made to understand them "in context." None of us ever appreciates being quoted by someone else "out of context." With regard to biblical interpretation, this means first of all that no biblical passage should be lifted from its place and transported into a discussion which is foreign to its original concern. That means that we pay close attention to the literary setting of each biblical passage, to the way in which it relates to the original paragraph, chapter, and book in which it is found. Thus we pay attention to its "context."

But the "context" of a biblical passage includes more than merely the literary setting on the page. Context also refers to the historical and social settings in which the words in question were written. For instance, when a given writer refers to "the president," we must know the time and place of writing, the precise period that is being discussed, and the social setting in question in order for us to determine which "president" is meant and which institution he or she presides over. "The wind blew the woman's hood off her head onto the hood of a car, and a hood came along and stole it." The precise definitions of the word "hood" in the previous sentence will depend on its historical and social contexts.

Therefore when we study the Scriptures we shall make an initial attempt to read the biblical material in its literary, historical, and social context. It is especially important in the case of the Book of Revelation to ask what it is that the author himself had in mind, rather than simply to make him say what we want him to say. What was the author's intention as he addressed his readers? What was their common situation which led him to write as he did?

I John, your brother, who share with you in Jesus the tribulation and the kingdom and the patient endurance, was on the island called Patmos on account of the word of God and the testimony of Jesus. (1:9)

The author identifies himself by name as "John" and as a "brother" to his readers, a partner with them "in Jesus." Furthermore, he shares with them "the tribulation and the kingdom and the patient endurance." So the common situation of the author and his readers is one of persecution, a situation in which they have been suffering for their commitment to "the word of God and the testimony of Jesus." The "tribulation," brought upon them because of their faithful witness, is for them a present reality.

The author himself writes from the island of Patmos, located just off the coast of Asia Minor (see the map on page vii). He does not specifically say that he has been forced to go there, although we may surmise as much from the connection with the reference to persecution in this verse. But we may not completely rule out the fact that he is on Patmos for missionary purposes. Yet he knows that his churches are under severe pressure, and he is concerned for them in this time of intense danger.

When he opened the fifth seal, I saw under the altar the souls of those who had been slain for the word of God and for the witness they had borne; they cried out with a loud voice, "O Sovereign Lord, holy and true, how long before thou wilt judge and avenge our blood on those who dwell upon the earth?" Then they were each given a white robe and told to rest a little longer, until the number of their fellow servants and their brethren should be complete, who were to be killed as they themselves had been. (6:9-11)

Then the dragon was angry with the woman, and went off to make war on the rest of her offspring, on those who keep the commandments of God and bear testimony to Jesus. (12:17)

And the beast was given a mouth uttering haughty and blasphemous words, and it was allowed to exercise authority for forty-two months. . . . Also it was allowed to make war on the saints and to conquer them. (13:5–7)

The author knows the situation of his readers well, and shares it with them. They have suffered humiliation, oppression, and martyrdom. Now he addresses them with a definite purpose:

> If any one has an ear, let him hear:
> If any one is to be taken captive,
>   to captivity he goes;
> if any one slays with the sword,
>   with the sword must he be slain.
> Here is a call for the endurance and faith
>   of the saints. (13:9–10)

The purpose of the author of the Book of Revelation, then, is to issue to his readers a message of encouragement, a call for endurance in their time of oppression. His writing is a message of hope that the forces of evil which are arrayed against them will not have the last word. The future belongs to God, and it is folly for any human being or for any human institution, no matter how powerful, to try to usurp God's control over it. The author's own aim, then, far from addressing himself to later generations, is to bring a word of hope to his readers in their own troubled times.

John of Patmos and His Churches

Who is this mysterious "John" who speaks to his churches from the island of Patmos? In Rev. 1:9 he identifies himself by name along with his place of writing, but no further information is given about him or about his specific relationship to his readers. We hear only in general terms that he is their "brother" who shares with them the persecution they are enduring. Who was "John of Patmos?"

Such a question is a historical question, and we must proceed as best we can to offer a historical answer. Whenever we ask questions about the past, we come face to face with our own limitations, for our answers are only as good as the data with which we have to work. If we are still uncertain about how many people were involved in the assassination of President Kennedy, which happened only two decades ago, then we must exercise great humility when we make judgments about events and persons of nineteen hundred years ago. Historical judgments are made only to the highest probability on the basis of the data which have come down to us. To return to our question: who was "John of Patmos"?

Church tradition has identified John of Patmos as Jesus' disciple John, the son of Zebedee and brother of James. But there is no way to verify the truth of this tradition. If fact, if one compares the vocabulary and the literary style of the Book of Revelation with other writings in the New Testament which have been attributed to the Zebedean John, one will find such great disparity as to render difficult the opinion that the same author is responsible for them all.

Furthermore, it is often pointed out that it would have been advantageous for our author to have referred to his apostolic authority, but nowhere in this writing does he claim to be an apostle, and the reference in Rev. 21:14 to "twelve names of the twelve apostles of the Lamb" seems not to include the author among the apostolic circle. There is also nothing in the Book of Revelation which indicates that the author knew Jesus during Jesus' ministry.

On the other hand, it is also pointed out that every leading church figure of the second century accepted that the apostle John, the disciple of Jesus, was the author of this writing. It was not until the third and fourth centuries that such authorship was called into question. The church historian Eusebius (writing about A.D. 312) thought that the author was not John the Apostle, but rather the famous John the Elder of Ephesus. This raises the possibility that there was some earlier confusion in the second century about persons who bore the same name of "John" and who were leaders in the church at the end of the first century. We do know that there existed some confusion among second-century fathers concerning first-century leaders named "Philip." A modern scholar has even raised the question of whether some of the material presented by our John of Patmos could actually have originated with another great apocalyptic "John" of the first century, namely, John the Baptist! But this latter suggestion has met with little agreement.

The result of all this is that we cannot with precision identify John of Patmos with any other famous "John" of the first-century church. This takes nothing away from our ability to evaluate and appreciate this writing. We do know the author's name and location, something which cannot be said for every other writing in the New Testament! Let it suffice for us simply to refer to our author as "John of Patmos."

In fact, that was sufficient for his churches. However, in their case no further explicit identification was necessary since he was evidently well known to them and they to him. "They" are seven churches in Asia Minor, and at the outset he addresses himself to them: "John to the seven churches that are in Asia" (1:4). In the first three chapters John shows himself to be well aware of the situation of each of these churches and gives expression to his deep concern for their spiritual and physical welfare. His concern is twofold: the internal condition of the churches and the external threat which they are facing.

The external threat is the persecution of the church by the Roman state, most likely under the Emperor Domitian, who ruled from A.D. 81–96. While there were other emperors, such as Nero (A.D. 54–68), who persecuted Christians, it was not until Domitian's reign that failure to honor the emperor as a god was a punishable political offense. The second-century church father Irenaeus places the time of writing of the Book of Revelation toward the end of Domitian's reign, a dating which most scholars of today still prefer.

But John also knows that this external threat posed by the Roman state will be difficult to withstand if the churches allow their internal condition to deteriorate further. The church at Ephesus is described as having abandoned "the love you had at first" (2:4). The churches of Smyrna, Pergamum, and Thyatira are harboring theological controversy and false teaching. Sardis looks good from the outside but is really dead inside (3:1), and Laodicea is a fence-sitter, neither hot nor cold (3:15).

John seems pleased only with conditions within the church at Philadelphia.

But why *seven* churches, and why *these* seven? First of all, it is most likely that John chooses to address these seven churches because they are the ones which stand directly under his influence and authority. However, we know that in this same geographical area these were not the only churches that were in existence at John's time. There were churches at Colossae, Hierapolis, Troas, Magnesia, and Tralles—churches who faced the same oppressive government with which the churches named by John had to contend. We have every right to assume that there were other churches in the same area and at this same time whose names we no longer know. Why these *seven*?

We shall soon come to see that the number seven in this writing has great symbolic force for the author. It is the number symbolic of completeness. Therefore by addressing seven churches he is also addressing the entire church as well, asking Christians beyond these particular seven to interact with the message he offers. Christians of every time and place are challenged by John to examine whether the internal conditions of their churches have prepared them for external pressure. Have we abandoned the love we had at first? Do we foster controversy and disreputable teaching? Looking good on the outside, are we really dead? Are we fence-sitters, neither hot nor cold? Such questions are directed by John to his churches, but when he says "seven" he means us as well.

Letter and Apocalypse

The Book of Revelation begins with the words, "The apocalypse (or revelation) of Jesus Christ, which God gave him to show to his servants what must soon take place . . . ." The English word "apocalypse" is a literal translation of the opening word in the Greek text, and therefore it is proper to refer to the Book of Revelation as the "Apocalypse." As we have already mentioned, the word "apocalypse" means "revelation" or "unveiling," and it is used elsewhere in the New Testament (see esp. Gal. 1:12 and 1 Cor. 14:6, 26), but never with regard to an entire writing.

By beginning with this word the author seems to be classifying his work with a whole range of writings called "apocalypses," which became popular in both Judaism and Christianity around the beginning of the Christian era. That means that apocalyptic literature is not originally a Christian form of writing, but was in use elsewhere, particularly in Judaism, before the rise of Christianity. (For a listing of such writings see Appendix A.)

Earlier we reviewed some of the general characteristics of apocalyptic literature for comparison with the interests of the Book of Revelation. We also suggested that we look for differences between the work of John of Patmos and the apocalyptic tradition which might help us discover the unique interests of John. By the time we have read ten verses into the Book of Revelation we have met up with one of these differences.

A general characteristic of apocalyptic literature is that the authors present their material in the words of an ancient figure of the past—for example, Daniel, Ezra, Baruch, Enoch, Moses, Abraham. The revelation is mediated by a heavenly being to a human recipient whose closeness to God enables him to see the secrets of the future which exist now in heaven but are the future for the earth and its peoples. Furthermore, these secrets are not for everyone, but are only to be transmitted to a chosen few (cf. Dan. 12:4, 9–10; 4 Ezra [2 Esdras] 14:45–47). Now how does the Book of Revelation differ from these traits in apocalyptic tradition?

First of all, the author of Revelation writes in his own name. He does not write in the name of a venerable figure of the ancient past, separated by the centuries from his readers, imparting an impersonal program for world history and its final end. For example, the words of Enoch are written "not for this generation, but for a remote one which is to come" (1 Enoch 1:2). By contrast, John of Patmos writes in his own name to people he knows, with whose situation he can identify: "I John, your brother, who share with you in Jesus the tribulation and the kingdom and the patient endurance, . . . " (1:9).

Second, he writes a *letter* in his own name—a letter to seven churches. His writing is a personal communication addressed to a particular readership with their particular circumstances in mind. "John to the seven churches that are in Asia" (1:4). This

unusual combination of letter and apocalypse will always remind
us to take the original author and his original readers seriously
and to let our interpretation begin there. The Book of Revelation
was intended first and foremost as a personal communication
between a particular author and people well known to him.

Third, this personal communication is not meant to be secre-
tive, reserved only for a chosen few. It is a personal communication and a public proclamation. In contrast to Dan. 12:4, in which
Daniel is told to "shut up the words, and seal the book, until the
time of the end," John of Patmos is told the opposite: "Do not
seal up the words of the prophecy of this book" (22:10). John
himself sees no restriction limiting his audience to a given group,
even only to the seven churches. At the very outset he relays a
beatitude without such restriction: "Blessed is he who reads
aloud the words of the prophecy, and blessed are those who hear,
and who keep what is written therein" (1:3). John's writing is a
personal communication and a public proclamation: a letter and
a prophecy.

It is interesting that so much of the New Testament is made up
of *letters*. The earliest writings in the New Testament are letters,
the letters of Paul. Paul wrote letters as a means of keeping in
contact with his congregations when he could not be physically
present with them. Some of his letters were written in order to
answer specific questions which had arisen within the congregations (cf. 1 Cor. 7:1). Some letters were written to thank the
churches for their support (cf. Phil. 4:10–20) or to encourage
them for future support (Rom. 15:22–29). One letter was written
on behalf of a runaway slave (Philemon).

Paul's letters were means of personal communication. And
Paul did not hesitate to let his own person surface. He can rejoice
with his readers (Phil. 2:18), weep with them (2 Cor. 2:4; 7:7),
show his frustration (Gal. 4:20) and even his anger (Phil. 3:2). In
every case it is true that the more we can know about the particular situation Paul is addressing, the more we can come to understand and appreciate his words—and then even apply them to
ourselves.

But it is precisely such an exercise which disturbs some
people. If we learn more about the human situations of the bibli-

cal writers, will we not think less of the Bible? If the Bible is the Word of God, why should we be concerned about the human situations out of which it arose? Will it not become too familiar? Will it not lose its power?

The answer lies in what God himself has chosen to do. He has chosen to get his work done through human beings: through Sarah the skeptic and Jacob the deceiver and Moses the outsider; through Rahab the harlot and Jeremiah the traitor; through Paul the persecutor and John the exile. The human dimension became so important to God that he entered into it himself. The Word became flesh.

Even Paul at first thought that if he could become less human he could do a better job for God. He could become a better missionary if his "thorn in the flesh" could be removed. But it was not removed, and Paul came to learn that God's power is made perfect in human weakness (2 Cor. 12:7–9). Only then could he write to the Thessalonians: "And we also thank God constantly for this, that when you received the word of God which you heard from us, you accepted it not as the word of men but as what it really is, the word of God, which is at work in you believers" (1 Thess. 2:13).

So as Paul did, the exile John also wrote a letter. But it is more than a letter. It is a "word of prophecy" to be read aloud in the churches (Rev. 1:3) as Paul's letters were (Col. 4:16). That means that this "prophecy" has little to do with foretelling the distant future, but rather with the proclamation of the Word of God for the present. "Prophecy" means intelligible preaching (see 1 Corinthians 14), and John of Patmos considers himself one of the prophets or preachers of the church (19:10; 22:9). He bears witness "to the word of God and to the testimony of Jesus Christ" (1:2).

This helps us better to understand what the word "apocalypse" or "revelation" means for John of Patmos. It is a means of personal communication among Christian believers which is, at the same time, the Word of God. It happens in the Christian worship assembly, as Paul once wrote: "how shall I benefit you unless I bring you some revelation or knowledge or prophecy or teaching?" (1 Cor. 14:6). "When you come together, each one has a hymn, a lesson, a revelation, a tongue, or an interpretation. Let all things be done for edification" (1 Cor. 14:26).

Apocalypse plus letter equals prophecy, a proclamation of the Word of God by a preacher to his congregation. John of Patmos brings something new, something unique, to that kind of writing called apocalyptic. It is a means of sharing the gospel with his own fellow believers.

Seeing and Hearing

John of Patmos sees and hears, and the hearing is every bit as important as the seeing: "I John am he who heard and saw these things. And when I heard and saw them, I fell down to worship . . ." (Rev. 22:8). Perhaps the hearing is even more important, for what John hears and sees he must further explain, and his explanation is to be *heard* by his audience. It is through hearing that they receive it as prophetic Word of God: "Blessed is he who reads aloud the words of the prophecy, and blessed are those who hear . . ." (1:3; cf. 22:18).

Hearing is important for John. For the God of the Old and New Testaments is a God who speaks. He is different from the other gods, who are seen and not heard. The presence of the other gods is manifested in symbol, in image, in idols, but not in speaking or hearing. The other gods are "idols of gold and silver and bronze and stone and wood, *which cannot either see or hear* . . ." (9:20, italics added).

So the God of Israel commanded that his people make of him no graven image (Exod. 20:4–5; Deut. 5:8–9). For such an image is something which is created by human beings over which they exercise their control and which remains at their disposal. They define the image, the symbol, the idol, and they have the last word over it. But no word comes from it other than what they want to hear.

Therefore hearing is important for the writers of the New Testament. Our relationship with God, said St. Paul, is not the result of our own doing but of our hearing with faith (Gal. 3:2, 5). For in hearing we have something given to us, something which begins outside of us, which we receive. Hearing with faith means we have received something which we did not initiate, for God is not at our disposal to define and to shape as we please. What we hear is the word which makes faith possible for us, the word of God's acceptance of us in Christ. "So faith comes from what is heard, and what is heard comes by the preaching of Christ" (Rom. 10:17).

Small wonder, then, that the Fourth Gospel speaks of Jesus as the *Word* made flesh, the ultimate communication of God among his people (John 1:1–18). If Jesus' disciples are to see anything they are to see in Jesus the Father who sent him (14:8–11), just as the Word they hear from Jesus comes from the Father (14:10, 24). The time of Jesus is a time of the Word, of listening and hearing: those who hear his Word and believe have eternal life (5:24). Those who insist on more than hearing are told: "Blessed are those who have not seen and yet believe" (20:29). And Paul had put it the same way: "we walk by faith, not by sight" (2 Cor. 5:7).

When reading the Book of Revelation we must remember, then, that what is seen is also to be heard. In fact, what is seen is the vehicle for what is heard. We are to hear not simply the symbolic imagery but the Word behind the symbol. For the symbol lies at our disposal to do with it what we wish. At our disposal, the conflict between the eagle and the bear can become a war between the United States and the Soviet Union, or a football game between Philadelphia and Chicago, or a boxing match between Muhammad Ali and Sonny Liston. But if we listen for the sound behind the symbols, we shall hear a word for all of us, a word which comes from beyond all of us, the Word of the gospel: "Worthy is Christ, the Lamb who was slain, whose blood set us free to be people of God!"

That is the song of the people of God at worship, the theme of the communal hymns of praise heard often in the Book of Revelation (cf. 4:11; 5:9, 12; 15:3). John begins and ends his writing in a worship setting, "in the Spirit on the Lord's day" (1:10) and with the eucharistic prayer *maranatha*, "Come, Lord Jesus!" (22:20; cf. 1 Cor. 11:26). The worship assembly is under the guidance of the Spirit of God, and therefore it is a time of witness and hearing, of celebrating the good news of God with the saints. It is a time of "revelation and knowledge and prophecy and teaching" (cf. 1 Cor. 14:6) offered among Christians to one another.

The "revelation" and the "prophecy" come to us through others present with us in worship. But the primary object of our attention is not the form of the revelation or of the prophecy or the person who mediates them. The function of the revelation and the prophecy is that of "witness to the word of God and to the testimony of Jesus" (Rev. 1:2), which will reveal and proclaim to us now the meaning of this world and of our place within it. In the setting of Christian worship we listen for the revealing and proclaiming word of him who is Alpha and Omega, who is and who was and who is to come (1:8). That word is not to be hidden, but heard (22:10). So we shall approach the Book of Revelation as listeners, as hearers with faith. To use one of John's favorite refrains, "he who has an ear, let him hear what the Spirit says to the churches" (2:7, 11, 17, 29; 3:6, 13, 22; cf. 13:9).

1
The Prologue

REV. 1:1-8

1 The revelation of Jesus Christ, which God gave him to show to his servants what must soon take place; and he made it known by sending his angel to his servant John, ²who bore witness to the word of God and the testimony of Jesus Christ, even to all that he saw. ³Blessed is he who reads aloud the words of the prophecy, and blessed are those who hear, and who keep what is written therein; for the time is near.

⁴John to the seven churches that are in Asia:

Grace to you and peace from him who is and who was and who is to come, and from the seven spirits who are before his throne, ⁵and from Jesus Christ the faithful witness, the firstborn of the dead, and the ruler of kings on earth.

To him who loves us and has freed us from our sins by his blood ⁶and made us a kingdom, priests to his God and Father, to him be glory and dominion for ever and ever. Amen. ⁷Behold, he is coming with the clouds, and every eye will see him, every one who pierced him; and all tribes of the earth will wail on account of him. Even so. Amen.

⁸"I am the Alpha and the Omega," says the Lord God, who is and who was and who is to come, the Almighty.

The Book of Revelation begins with a prologue (1:1–8) and concludes with an epilogue (22:6–21). Both sections are closely related to each other in terms of style, vocabulary, and subject matter. Both sections contain a number of smaller subunits which give the impression that each section comprises a rather artificial combination of individual statements rather loosely strewn together. But this initial impression can be modified by a closer look at both sections.

In the prologue the various subunits fall into the following pattern:

1:1-2   Introduction to the book
1:3   Beatitudes
1:4-5c   Salutation
1:5d-6   Doxology
1:7   Text
1:8   Theme

Within this pattern we can detect an attempt to combine two distinct interests, namely, the literary and the liturgical. John of Patmos has received a message which he now must proclaim. But he must write it first and then let it be heard in the churches (1:3, 11). This mixture of literary and liturgical elements is seen in 1:4-5c, which contains the usual manner of address in ancient letters now elaborated by liturgical-confessional terminology. This movement between the literary and the liturgical is necessitated by John's desire to *write* a *prophecy*, that is, to write something which should be heard by the Christian community at worship. It is a problem which confronts every preacher today: *writing* a sermon which is to be *spoken*—and then afterwards being asked for a copy of what has been spoken.

John's writing takes the form of a letter. The function of a letter is that of a means of communication between people who are separated from each other. John is separated from his churches (1:9), and it is very likely that the way he addresses them in 1:4-8 is the way he has addressed them before when he was physically present in their midst. He knows that they are still assembling together (1:3), and he can envision their worship practices. Perhaps his habitual homiletical style is reflected in 1:4-8, and he uses it as a further means of identification to allow his audience the certainty of knowing that the one who addresses them here is the one who has addressed them before. "Grace to you and peace from him who is and who was and who is to come . . ." (1:4).

The dual salutation, "Grace and peace," is found at the beginning of every one of Paul's letters, and it soon became a traditional means of formal greeting among Christians (cf. also 1 and 2 Pet. 1:2). It speaks of and asks for the grace and peace which comes from God and reminds us of the favor and acceptance God has extended to us. To this dual salutation John adds a phrase identifying the God who grants grace and peace to his people: he is the one "who was and who is and who is to come." This identification, which John has built out of the name of God given in Exod. 3:14–15, is used again in Rev. 1:8 and 4:8 and forms a standard against which the false gods are measured (cf. 17:8). "Grace and peace" are also to come from the "seven spirits who are before his throne," which could be a reference to the presence of the one Holy Spirit in each of the angels of the seven churches (cf. 3:1; 1:20), and from Jesus, the faithful witness, risen and exalted.

This identification of Jesus as risen and exalted is amplified in the doxology which follows in 1:5d–6. The one who is risen and exalted is always the crucified, the one who was pierced (1:7). This identification is extremely important for John: the triumphant Jesus is always the Lamb who was slain (5:6, 12; 13:8), whose cross has won the victory and liberated us from the forces of sin and death (1:5; 7:14; 12:11; 17:14; 19:13). It is by the victory of his cross that we are made a people now set apart for God's own special use, "a kingdom, priests" (1:6). It is to the crucified Christ that "glory and dominion" now belong (1:6).

We have designated Rev. 1:7 as a "text," that is, as a basis for John's proclamation which is to follow. It is a "text" because the verse is constructed out of two Old Testament passages, namely, Dan. 7:13, which speaks of the one coming on the clouds of heaven, and Zech. 12:10, which speaks of those who would, on the day of the Lord, "look on him whom they pierced" and "mourn for him." John underscores the point of 1:5d again: the Christ who returns at the end of time will be recognized by everyone as the one who was crucified.

The theme in 1:8 is comprehensive for John's entire writing: "'I am the Alpha and the Omega,' says the Lord God, who is and who was and who is to come, the Almighty." This is God's own self-designation (cf. also 21:6, 13) and is meant to recall God's immortality as contrasted with human mortality. Alpha and Omega are the first and last letters of the Greek alphabet, the "beginning and the end" (21:6), and the time in between is reflected in the additional designation, "who is and who was and who is to come."

The prologue, with its combination of literary and liturgical elements, has prepared us to enter with John of Patmos into the Christian worship assembly, to hear and see what John "in the Spirit on the Lord's day" (1:10) heard and saw: his prophetic call (1:9–20), his prophetic address (2:1—3:22), and his prophetic vision (4:1—22:5).

2

The Prophetic Call

REV. 1:9–20

⁹I John, your brother, who share with you in Jesus the tribulation and the kingdom and the patient endurance, was on the island called Patmos on account of the word of God and the testimony of Jesus. ¹⁰I was in the Spirit on the Lord's day, and I heard behind me a loud voice like a trumpet ¹¹saying, "Write what you see in a book and send it to the seven churches, to Ephesus and to Smyrna and to Per'gamum and to Thyati'ra and to Sardis and to Philadelphia and to Laodice'a."

¹²Then I turned to see the voice that was speaking to me, and on turning I saw seven golden lampstands, ¹³and in the midst of the lampstands one like a son of man, clothed with a long robe and with a golden girdle round his breast; ¹⁴his head and his hair were white as white wool, white as snow; his eyes were like a flame of fire, ¹⁵his feet were like burnished bronze, refined as in a furnace, and his voice was like the sound of many waters; ¹⁶in his right hand he held seven stars, from his mouth issued a sharp two-edged sword, and his face was like the sun shining in full strength.

¹⁷When I saw him, I fell at his feet as though dead. But he laid his right hand upon me, saying, "Fear not, I am the first and the last, ¹⁸and the living one; I died, and behold I am alive for evermore, and I have the keys of Death and Hades. ¹⁹Now write what you see, what is and what is to take place hereafter. ²⁰As for the mystery of the seven stars which you saw in my right hand, and the seven golden lampstands, the seven stars are the angels of the seven churches and the seven lampstands are the seven churches

John of Patmos understands himself to be one of the prophets or preachers of the church (19:10; 22:9). Like the Old Testament prophets, John records his call to prophesy, for it is very important for the biblical prophets to state at the outset that the word they proclaim is not their own word. It is a word which they have been given, a word from God to God's people.

It is a very serious claim—to speak in the name of God. Those who do so must not take their task lightly, and they must reckon with the possibility, on the part of their hearers, of hostility, rejection, and even expulsion from the community they feel called to address. But once called, the prophet cannot remain silent. As Amos wrote: "The lion has roared; who will not fear? The Lord God has spoken; who can but prophesy?" (Amos 3:8). It is not ambition which drives the prophet to speak on God's behalf, not a sense of self-importance. It is simply a matter of necessity. As St. Paul said: "For if I preach the gospel, that gives me no ground for boasting. For necessity is laid upon me. Woe to me if I do not preach the gospel!" (1 Cor. 9:16). The call to speak for God does not bring the recipient immediate elation, but instead signals the beginning of struggle, self-doubt, and deep feelings of personal unworthiness.

"Woe is me!" exclaimed the prophet Isaiah at his call. "For I am lost; for I am a man of unclean lips . . . ; for my eyes have seen the King, the Lord of hosts!" (6:5). When Jeremiah is told that the Lord had singled him out for his prophetic mission, he hesitates, saying, "Ah, Lord God! Behold, I do not know how to speak, for I am only a youth" (1:6).

But it is precisely the sinful Isaiah and the youthful Jeremiah whom God chooses to send to his people. What makes them prophets is neither their mortality nor their maturity but the God who forgives and empowers them. So the Lord said to Jeremiah, "Do not say, 'I am only a youth'; for to all to whom I send you you shall go, and whatever I command you you shall speak. Be not afraid of them, for I am with you to deliver you" (Jer. 1:7–8).

When John of Patmos, the exile, received his call to proclaim the Word of God and the testimony of Jesus, he experienced what prophets before him had experienced. He was knocked flat on his face (1:17)—no chin held high above reproach, no flight into the spiritual stratosphere, no know-it-all grabbing at the prophetic vocation. He felt like he was dead. Only then was he ready for ordination, only then ready to receive the Word which he in turn was to preach: "Fear not, I am the first and the last, and the living one; I died, and behold I am alive for evermore, and I have the keys of Death and Hades" (1:17–18).

As an exile, John had experienced Death and Hades. The powers of death and hell had surrounded him, bringing oppression and martyrdom to his loved ones in the churches and sending him packing to Patmos. From the shadows of his earthly existence came the loud voices of the hostile powers, challenging Christian commitment and causing the oppressed to ask: Why have we experienced such suffering? How long will it continue? Will the church survive? Are the people of God forgotten?

But John hears another voice, one which offers an answer to the puzzling mystery of his desperate existence: "I died, and behold I am alive for evermore, and I have the keys of Death and Hades" (1:18). And John is told to write just that to the churches. Death is not the last word in their vocabulary, and Hades is not the sole prospect of their future, for the One whose voice stands clear and distinct above the shadows has conquered them both. He is the one who died and is now alive.

That is the message John hears, and he hears it in the midst of the Christian community at worship. He is "in the Spirit on the Lord's day" (1:10) where the word of Christ's triumph is proclaimed, and the voice that he hears comes from the midst of the lampstands (1:13), that is, from among the churches (1:20). God has not forgotten his people. The ascended and exalted Christ is not absent but stands among his own, and those who hear with faith will see him in their midst. What they see is a powerful sight (1:13–16), a sight far beyond any earthly description of one at whose feet Death and Hades lie broken.

No one earthly description can suffice for this victor. It is Daniel's "Son of Man" in high-priestly attire, the "Ancient of Days" in the splendor of Ezekiel's cherubim (cf. Dan. 7:9, 13; Ezek. 1:7). His only weapon is his word (cf. Isa. 11:4), his face comparable only to the sun. But the most profound thing about this sight is the way it identifies itself: "I died! And behold I am alive for evermore!"

In the midst of the church at worship John finds the key to his earthly existence, in the Word of him who unravels the churches' torment and says to them: "Fear not!" The crucified and risen

Christ is the means by which the churches are to interpret their past, present, and future. The churches are no longer to fear the powers of death and hell because their eyes are fixed on the one who died and is now alive. The hostile powers no longer stand over them because of the one who is in their midst.

So at the beginning of his sermon, John can remind his churches of "him who loves us and has freed us" (1:5). Freed from anxiety about present or future, freed from useless speculation and feverish expectation, the churches now hear the Word of him who says, "Fear not! I am the first and the last." The coming one is the one who has been here before. The coming one is the same one who said, "Peace be with you. As the Father has sent me, even so I send you" (John 20:21). The coming one is the same one who said, "It is not for you to know times or seasons" (Acts 1:7). We do not need to know, for the coming one is the same one who said, "My sheep hear my voice, and *I know them*" (John 10:27, italics added)!

Therefore John's message to his churches can properly begin with the words "Grace to you and peace": from the Father, who is and was and is to come, Alpha and Omega; from the Spirit, who gives his gifts to each of the churches as he wills; and from the Son, who holds the unity of the churches in his hand (1:4–5, 20).

3
The Letters to the Seven Churches

REV. 2:1—3:22

By beginning his writing with his call to prophesy John has stated that his message to the churches is not his own word, but a word he himself has received. It is a word of prophecy, a word of preaching, a proclamation of the Word of God. It is a revelation given to him by God which has a direct bearing on the immediate life of John's churches: "to show to his servants what must soon take place" (1:1). At the close of his writing John reminds his readers of this again: they are to keep this proclamation before them, for it is spoken to their immediate situation (22:10).

Therefore the proclamation or revelation begins with letters to seven churches whose immediate situation is well known to the author and to the one who walks among them (1:20—2:1). As each church is addressed it hears the words: "I know your works . . . ," or "I know your tribulation . . . ," or "I know where you dwell." Then follows a description of conditions which exist within the life of each church. But each church is addressed within the context of a prophetic address to *seven* churches, and we shall see how important the number seven is throughout the entire Book of Revelation. The number seven is the number for completeness, and by addressing each church within a complex of seven letters the author is addressing the whole church as well.

This means that all seven churches are to listen to what is said to each one. The whole church is to hear what is said to one church in one given place. For the church in Ephesus is *the church*—in Ephesus. That is, the positives and the negatives of church life in Ephesus are the same elsewhere, and what hap-

41

pens elsewhere happens also in Ephesus. The churches can
learn from each other.

That is where we come in. Every single manifestation of
church life in these seven churches can surface among the
churches of our own time. Therefore John's address can be received as Word of God to us all. And as we learn from the
churches addressed in John's letters, we can also learn from each
other.

Therefore John's letters to the seven churches comprise more
than simply a prologue or an introduction to the Book of Revelation. For the subject of the revelation is the presence (or absence)
of Jesus in the life of the churches. The subject of the revelation
is not a periodization of world history or a philosophy of time, but
a Word from one who walks among the churches, challenging
them to live the gospel in an often hostile world. The subject of
the revelation in the life of the churches, of the whole church, is a
call for the endurance of the saints (13:10; 14:12). The resources
John uses and the imagery he employs are directed toward one
purpose: to cause us to ask whether in *our* church the presence of
Jesus Christ is seen and heard, celebrated and proclaimed, envisioned and lived. And not tomorrow, next year, or at the end of
this century—but *now!*

EPHESUS

2 "To the angel of the church in Ephesus write: 'The words of him who
holds the seven stars in his right hand, who walks among the seven
golden lampstands.

2"'I know your works, your toil and your patient endurance, and how
you cannot bear evil men but have tested those who call themselves
apostles but are not, and found them to be false; ³I know you are enduring patiently and bearing up for my name's sake, and you have not
grown weary. ⁴But I have this against you, that you have abandoned the
love you had at first. ⁵Remember then from what you have fallen, repent
and do the works you did at first. If not, I will come to you and remove
your lampstand from its place, unless you repent. ⁶Yet this you have, you
hate the works of the Nicola'itans, which I also hate. ⁷He who has an ear,
let him hear what the Spirit says to the churches. To him who conquers I
will grant to eat of the tree of life, which is in the paradise of God.'"

Ephesus is addressed first, very likely because it is the nearest of the seven to Patmos. The opening line, "To the angel of the church in Ephesus" (2:1) reflects the ancient idea that each of the angels of God held responsibility for the administration of one nation (cf. Deut. 32:8; Dan. 10:20–21; 12:1). The one who "for a little while was made lower than the angels" (Heb. 2:9) now holds them in his hand (Rev. 2:1). It is he who has conquered and to whom the administering angels are responsible. That means that the administration of the churches—bishops, clergy, and laity—are responsible to their Lord, whose victory over the hostile worldly powers is already won (1:18).

The words addressed to the church in Ephesus are from its victorious Lord, present now among his churches (2:1). There are good things to be said about Ephesus. It is an active church, a patient, steadfast church (2:2–3). But it also is a fallen church in need of repentance (2:5). For in its zeal to purge itself of false teachers, it has succumbed to lovelessness (2:2, 4). It now has a reputation as a great heresy-hunting church, but it has missed the point of the gospel: it has abandoned love. Hating works is one thing, but hating people is another (2:6). And if the victorious Lord is forced to choose between truth and love, he will choose love. He does not need an orthodox church in Ephesus, but a loving one, and if this church does not return to love he will not allow it to continue (2:5). The one who has conquered by means of his own love of sinners will not be represented by zealots who hate. His promise of life is to those who conquer hatred as he has (2:7).

This is not a word just for Ephesus, but for the other six as well, and thus for the church in every time and place: "He who has an ear, let him hear what the Spirit says to the *churches*" (2:7, italics added). So if we want to hear, for Ephesus substitute New York, Philadelphia, Minneapolis, St. Louis, Canterbury, or Rome, and we shall have a word to the churches. It is a word which asks us whether we are more responsive to the voices of hatred than to the voices of love. If to the voices of hatred, then what right do we have to represent the one who gave himself for us because he loved us (1:5)?

For the church in Ephesus the coming of Jesus may pose a

crisis. But it is very important to recognize that the coming of
Jesus referred to here is not his coming at the end of time. Jesus
will come to this church, but time and history will continue. The
question is whether this church will continue! The advent of
Jesus mentioned in 2:5 is not his coming to judge the world but
his coming to judge this church in Ephesus. If this church does
not return to the love it had at first, the world will continue but
this church will not. So the members of this church need not
engage in feverish speculation about the end of the world. Their
immediate task is to discover whether their current church life is
consistent with their Lord's presence *now*. If not, then repentance, that is, return, is in order (2:5). For Christ's Parousia, his
presence, is *now*, and it brings with it both blessing and demand.
Chirst's Parousia has to do not only with our expectations but
with his expectations as well.

SMYRNA

[8]"And to the angel of the church in Smyrna write: 'The words of the
first and the last, who died and came to life.

[9]" 'I know your tribulation and your poverty (but you are rich) and the
slander of those who say that they are Jews and are not, but are a
synagogue of Satan. [10]Do not fear what you are about to suffer. Behold,
the devil is about to throw some of you into prison, that you may be
tested, and for ten days you will have tribulation. Be faithful unto death,
and I will give you the crown of life. [11]He who has an ear, let him hear
what the Spirit says to the churches. He who conquers shall not be hurt
by the second death.'"

The opening words of the letter to the church at Smyrna again
identify the source of the revelation as Christ himself. The introductory statements to each of the churches employ imagery used
of Jesus throughout the entire Book of Revelation, beginning
with Chapter 1. This is one of the ways by which the author
weaves the various parts of the book together.

The church in Smyrna has experienced hatred—from those
who should have been friends but who have turned hostile (2:9).
This church has experienced rejection by friends and separation
from a religious fellowship it had formerly known. In the Roman

Empire of the first century, Judaism had the privileged status of a legal religion; when Christians were forced to leave the synagogues because of their new faith, they became vulnerable to official state penalties for holding illegal beliefs. Christians in Smyrna could now no longer count on the protection offered them by fellowship with the synagogue.

So the church in Smyrna has nothing to look forward to but hardship, persecution, and death. Even into the second century this church was subjected to violent persecution, as it witnessed the martyrdom of its bishop, Polycarp, in A.D. 155. To all external appearances this church looks poor and without a future. But in actuality the people of this church are rich (2:9). For they know what death is, for in their baptism they have already died with Christ whose victory removes from them the fear of another death. Because of their Lord, their death in this world is not the last word; therefore they need not fear another death beyond it (2:11; cf. 20:6, 14–15 and our comments on p. 114). Their Lord is the one who died and now lives, and his future is now their future (2:10).

This word of consolation to Smyrna is also a word of consolation to all the churches. The church of Christ has not been left alone in its times of testing but has been given resources with which to deal with the hostile powers of this world. The presence of the victorious Lord in word and sacrament is his promise of a future for his own.

PERGAMUM

[12]"And to the angel of the church in Per'gamum write: 'The words of him who has the sharp two-edged sword.

[13]" 'I know where you dwell, where Satan's throne is; you hold fast my name and you did not deny my faith even in the days of An'tipas my witness, my faithful one, who was killed among you, where Satan dwells. [14]But I have a few things against you: you have some there who hold the teaching of Balaam, who taught Balak to put a stumbling block before the sons of Israel, that they might eat food sacrificed to idols and practice immorality. [15]So you also have some who hold the teaching of the Nicola'itans. [16]Repent then. If not, I will come to you soon and war against them with the sword of my mouth. [17]He who has an ear, let him

hear what the Spirit says to the churches. To him who conquers I will give some of the hidden manna, and I will give him a white stone, with a new name written on the stone which no one knows except him who receives it.'"

The experience of the church at Pergamum has been common to the church of every age: external pressure from the government and internal pressure from its own members to conform to the wishes of the state. Pergamum had been a city of great wealth and splendor, and in 133 B.C. it became the seat of government for the Roman province of Asia. In 29 B.C. a great temple was built in honor of Rome and Caesar Augustus, making it an important center for the practice of emperor worship. But now the church at Pergamum was vulnerable, for by refusing to engage in the official civic religious exercises its members could be branded as unpatriotic.

Earlier, in 1 Cor. 10:20, St. Paul had written that what pagans sacrifice to idols is actually being offered to demons. So now John of Patmos can refer to the imperial cult and its temple at Pergamum as "Satan's throne," the place "where Satan dwells" (2:13). The pressure of government-controlled religion had resulted in the martyrdom of one of the members of the Pergamum church (2:13), and John acknowledges the church's steadfastness in the face of such violence against it.

But now there are some within the church who wish to compromise with the official religion of the empire. They feel that they have more in common with the government than they do with their fellow Christians who have resisted it. They are like Balaam (cf. Num. 25:1–3; 31:16), who encouraged Israel to practice idolatry and immorality. Perhaps they reasoned that Christians in Pergamum should participate in some phases of Roman religion only to show their patriotism and thereby to reduce official hostility against the church.

Such strategy is to be rejected as disreputable teaching which Christians in Pergamum must not heed. They are instead to listen to the one whose only weapon is his word. The one who walks among them and speaks his word to them addresses them with the sword of his mouth (2:12, 16). The risen Christ is present among his churches in his word, which is all the churches need for the securing of their future. If the churches neglect the word of Christ, then that same word will be used against them (2:16), for it alone, not human compromise with civic religion, has the authority and power to guarantee the churches' future (2:17). Once again, the coming of Christ with which this church should be concerned is not his future coming at the end of time, but his coming in his word. The church's expectation about Christ is now secondary to Christ's expectations about this church.

The message to Pergamum asks every Christian congregation of every age whether its witness to its immediate society has retained its evangelical sharpness. Has our testimony to Christ become dulled by narrowness and rigidity or by the casual acceptance of the shallow values of a materialistic culture? Has our Christian witness become muted by our allowing the notion of patriotism to take precedence over our calling to manifest the presence of Christ in our world? "I have not come to bring peace, but a sword," said Jesus (Matt. 10:34), and that sword is a Word also to the churches. It is two-edged, for both the world and the church.

THYATIRA

[18]"And to the angel of the church in Thyati'ra write: 'The words of the Son of God, who has eyes like a flame of fire, and whose feet are like burnished bronze.

[19]" 'I know your works, your love and faith and service and patient endurance, and that your latter works exceed the first. [20]But I have this against you, that you tolerate the woman Jez'ebel, who calls herself a prophetess and is teaching and beguiling my servants to practice immorality and to eat food sacrificed to idols. [21]I gave her time to repent, but she refuses to repent of her immorality. [22]Behold, I will throw her on a sickbed, and those who commit adultery with her I will throw into great tribulation, unless they repent of her doings; [23]and I will strike her children dead. And all the churches shall know that I am he who searches mind and heart, and I will give to each of you as your works deserve. [24]But to the rest of you in Thyati'ra, who do not hold this teaching, who have not learned what some call the deep things of Satan, to you I say, I do not lay upon you any other burden; [25]only hold fast what you have, until I come. [26]He who conquers and who keeps my works until the end, I will give him power over the nations, [27]and he shall rule them with a rod of iron, as when earthen pots are broken in

pieces, even as I myself have received power from my Father; [28]and I will give him the morning star. [29]He who has an ear, let him hear what the Spirit says to the churches.'"

What is said to the church at Thyatira parallels what was said to Pergamum, but with a little more particularity. The city of Thyatira was a prospering industrial city known especially for the many trade guilds that flourished there. In Acts 16:14–15 we hear of the Thyatiran businesswoman, Lydia, who responded to the preaching of Paul and Silas in Philippi and evidently opened her house there as a meeting place or house-church for the Christian community. Evidence for the network of guilds in Thyatira comes from various inscriptions mentioning bakers, potters, linen and leather workers, dyers, tanners, slave dealers, and bronzesmiths.

In the messages to Ephesus, Pergamum, and Thyatira, we meet up with a thorny theological controversy which raged throughout the Hellenistic mission churches of the first century. One side of this controversy is depicted in these letters by the symbolic names Balaam (2:14), Jezebel (2:20), and the Nicolaitans (2:7, 15). The first two names refer to Old Testament figures while the third name, Nicolaitans, is a Greek word whose meaning ("conqueror of the people") is very similar to the meaning of the Hebrew word Balaam ("consumer of the people"). All three names are connected in these letters to immorality and the eating of food sacrificed to idols. Very likely the names referred to the same group of Christians which engaged in these two practices.

Many scholars believe that the issue has to do with Christian freedom from the laws of the Old Testament. Certainly the early church eventually recognized its freedom in Christ from obligatory observance of the kosher food laws. However, it did not recognize such freedom with regard to sexual morality: promiscuity was rejected and chaste monogamous relationships and chaste celibacy were maintained (cf. 1 Corinthians 7; Heb. 13:4). So the issue in the controversy behind these letters is more than Christian freedom.

In Corinth some Christians dealt with the world not by obligatory withdrawal from it but by obligatory involvement in it. These Christians felt that those who had come to faith in Christ were obligated to carry on the fight against the evil powers of this world by meeting them on their own turf, by frequenting the brothels (1 Cor. 6:15–20) and pagan temples (8:7–13). By doing so they claimed to be "the strong," while other Christians who disagreed were "the weak." It was therefore the responsibility of "the strong" to perform every kind of action to show Christian superiority over false gods and thus to break the power of this world over the believer. There was no temptation which could overcome "the strong," and one of their slogans is reflected in 1 Cor. 10:13, a slogan which Paul restates and then uses in the opposite direction: "Therefore, my beloved, shun the worship of idols" (10:14).

The reply to Paul would be based on the Christian confessions that "an idol has no real existence" and that "there is no God but one" (1 Cor. 8:4). This frees Christians, or better *obliges* Christians, to witness the superiority of their faith by participating in pagan religious observances without fear of being overcome by a "false god" which, in fact, does not even exist.

At Thyatira this controversy would have its place within the context of the celebrations held by the trade guilds. Christian members of the trade guilds were confronted with the problem of their participation in celebrations which included acts of worship toward the emperor as a god, eating food sacrificed to idols and then served at the guild meetings and receptions, and contacts with local cult prostitutes. Some Christians would participate simply for economic reasons in order to maintain their professional standing in the guilds, while others had based their participation on theological reasons (as stated above), claiming to have a special spiritual knowledge about "the deep things of God" (cf. 1 Cor. 2:10).

John of Patmos responds by saying that behind such claims are nothing other than "the deep things of Satan" (2:24). This reminds us of Paul's point that an idol represents not something divine as much as something demonic, and that participation in sacrificial worship, even if it is an attempt to confront the demons on their own ground, is in effect a recognition of the power of the demons as hosts of the celebrations (1 Cor. 10:20–21).

Pergamum and Thyatira are told that not just anything goes in the Christian church. These congregations exist as witnesses to the presence of their victorious Lord, the Son of God (2:18). He is not to be confused with or easily substituted by others who claim divine sonship, either the emperor in Pergamum's imperial cult or the local Thyatiran deity Apollo Tyrimnos. When Christian witness is dulled by easy accommodation to the world around it, Christians must be confronted and cleansed by the Word of their Lord. They do not exist to promulgate esoteric doctrines which divide the church (2:24). They already have the gospel, and the risen Christ says to them: "I do not lay upon you any other burden; only hold fast what you have, until I come" (2:24–25).

SARDIS

3 "And to the angel of the church in Sardis write: 'The words of him who has the seven spirits of God and the seven stars.

"'I know your works; you have the name of being alive, and you are dead. ²Awake, and strengthen what remains and is on the point of death, for I have not found your works perfect in the sight of my God. ³Remember then what you received and heard; keep that, and repent. If you will not awake, I will come like a thief, and you will not know at what hour I will come upon you. ⁴Yet you have still a few names in Sardis, people who have not soiled their garments; and they shall walk with me in white, for they are worthy. ⁵He who conquers shall be clad thus in white garments, and I will not blot his name out of the book of life; I will confess his name before my Father and before his angels. ⁶He who has an ear, let him hear what the Spirit says to the churches.'"

The church at Sardis receives the harshest criticism offered to the seven churches. This church presents a picture which is not altogether unfamiliar to us. It is, as one commentator has said, "the perfect model of inoffensive Christianity." It has a great reputation in its community for being a live, active church, but behind the facade this church is dead (3:1). Sardis is a pathetic charade, a church going through the motions but with little substance to its witness. It has fooled everyone, including itself, for it cannot distinguish any longer between real Christian witness and useless religiosity.

There is only one person who has anything against this church.

Unfortunately, that one person is the very Lord this church is called to proclaim! In Sardis, Christian identity has been redefined in terms of comfortable accommodation to its surrounding culture, to the point where Christian discipleship has lost its creative and distinctive prophetic edge.

So now their Lord calls them to awake out of their sleep, to repent, and to remember the gospel (3:2–3). And we can imagine the utterly astonished response: "Awake? Who, us? Repent? Who, me? But look at all we've accomplished! Look at all we're doing! Everyone else tells us what a first-rate operation we have here! Everyone else keeps telling us what a perfect church we are!" But that is all irrelevant, for the one whose opinion really counts is not convinced: you may think otherwise, but "*I* have not found your works perfect in the sight of my God" (3:2, italics added).

To a church slumbering so deeply, the advent of Christ will come as a crisis. He will come to them when they least expect it, as the city of Sardis had experienced the stealthy attack of the Persians in 546 B.C. and the Syrians in 218 B.C., who had surprised Sardis like thieves in the night (3:3). He will come to look for those whose names he can own before God (3:4–5), whose identity has not been redefined on their own terms.

Not everyone in the church at Sardis has been slumbering. There are still a few whose identity has been defined by Christ crucified, their lives patterned after the cross of their Lord. Their garments are white (3:4), that is, they openly bear witness to the fact that they have been washed "in the blood of the Lamb" (7:14). They bear witness by their lives that they have been redeemed by Christ the crucified. Such identification is reinforced by the symbol that their names are written in the "book of life" (3:5). And in 21:27 we learn that the "book of life" belongs to the Lamb who was slain.

Those whose identity has been determined by the cross of Christ will not be surprised by the sudden advent of Christ. For just as they have openly confessed Christ's name before others in this world, so will Christ confess their names before God (3:5). This promise recalls an important word of Jesus in the Gospel of Mark (8:38), where the context has to do with the identity of both Jesus and his followers. The disciples find it difficult to accept

Jesus' own definition of his messiahship in terms of his cross
(8:27–33) and, therefore, difficult to accept his call to discipleship
in terms of that cross (8:34–38).

The risen Christ, the Lamb who was slain, will not be ashamed
to confess his own before God (3:5). His own are the ones who
have not been ashamed of him, of Christ crucified. They are the
ones who see in Jesus' cross God's own judgment on the standards of this world, and who have chosen to live not according to
those standards but as disciples of the one who died and was
raised.

PHILADELPHIA

7"And to the angel of the church in Philadelphia write: 'The words of
the holy one, the true one, who has the key of David, who opens and no
one shall shut, who shuts and no one opens.

8" 'I know your works. Behold, I have set before you an open door,
which no one is able to shut; I know that you have but little power, and
yet you have kept my word and have not denied my name. 9Behold, I
will make those of the synagogue of Satan who say that they are Jews
and are not, but lie—behold, I will make them come and bow down
before your feet, and learn that I have loved you. 10Because you have
kept my word of patient endurance, I will keep you from the hour of trial
which is coming on the whole world, to try those who dwell upon the
earth. 11I am coming soon; hold fast what you have, so that no one may
seize your crown. 12He who conquers, I will make him a pillar in the
temple of my God; never shall he go out of it, and I will write on him the
name of my God, and the name of the city of my God, the new Jerusalem
which comes down from my God out of heaven, and my own new name.
13He who has an ear, let him hear what the Spirit says to the churches.' "

Ancient Philadelphia was a prosperous city with an economy
based on agriculture, industry, and commerce. Situated at the
eastern end of a valley leading down to the Aegean Sea, the city
was founded as a way station for the spread of Greek culture, and
it became an important link on trade routes leading eastward to
the provinces of Lydia and Phrygia. Philadelphia was known as
"the gateway to the East."

A major problem for the city was that it had been built near a
geological fault line and was subjected to frequent earthquakes,

several of which had devastated the city. After the destructive quake of A.D. 17, the city was rebuilt with aid from Rome. To show its appreciation, it changed its name to honor the emperor under whose auspices the relief had been sent. This great attachment to Rome also meant the growing popularity of emperor worship in Philadelphia shown by an increasing number of temples constructed for the practice of the imperial cult.

These conditions are reflected in the words of praise John of Patmos transmits to the church in Philadelphia: "Behold, I have set before you an open door, which no one is able to shut; I know that you have but little power, and yet you have kept my word and have not denied my name" (3:8). "He who conquers, I will make him a pillar in the temple of my God; . . . and I will write on him the name of my God, and the name of the city of my God, the new Jerusalem which comes down from my God out of heaven, and my own new name" (3:12).

Philadelphia is praised because this church has not succumbed to the pressures of its environment. John has nothing negative to say about this church, and what he does say reflects the kind of pressures which its members have patiently withstood.

First, they have been pressured by the official religion of the Roman state. But the members of the church at Philadelphia had decided not to walk through the doors of the imperial cult. Now they are shut out of the positions of political power and social esteem in the city, especially since they have maintained their adherence to a faith not officially recognized as a legal religion by the government.

Second, they have been deserted by their friends. They had not sought separate status from their fellow believers in the God of Israel (3:9) but had been expelled because of their belief in Jesus as the Messiah (3:7). Like Christians in Smyrna (2:9) they had experienced rejection, separation from the traditions dear to them, and they were being told that their faith was not a genuine one. Those who should have been their friends were now shutting them out of their confessional circles. But their access to their Lord had not been disrupted, and this church under pressure hears "The words of the holy one, the true one, who has the

key of David, who opens and no one shall shut, who shuts and no
one opens" (3:7). "Behold, I have set before you an open door"
(3:8).

This word of the gospel to a church under pressure is at the
same time a word of challenge to those churches which do not
feel such pressure. In Philadelphia's time of trial—persecution
by foe and rejection by friend—it has patiently endured (3:10).
This church has not forsaken Christ, and therefore when a
greater time of trial comes Christ will not forsake this church.
Their faithfulness to Christ means Christ's faithfulness to them to
see them through any time of crisis and testing.

This good news remains a challenge to all the churches in
every time and place. It asks us to discover where our allegiance
really is. With whom do we identify—with the church under
pressure or with the ones who pressure the church? When we
read accurate reports of the persecution of Christians in our
world today, would we rather identify with their persecutors?
Would we accept John's words about the "synagogue of Satan" in
ancient Philadelphia but not raise our voice against official religious establishments which justify racial segregation by saying
that the primary task of the church does not include reconcilia-
tion between human beings?

Now our reading of Revelation starts coming closer to home!
As long as we can play speculative games about the predictabil-
ity of its contents we can keep the Word of God within it at a
distance from us. But if we read it for what it is meant to be,
namely, a prophecy, a proclamation of God's Word, then it will
not remain at a distance. It will, as St. Paul said, disclose the
secrets of our hearts and call us to account (1 Cor. 14:25). The
Book of Revelation asks us where our priorities are and whether
in the church, our church, Christ is present or absent. Is the name
proclaimed by our church its own name or the name of the state
or a name not bound by the institutions of this world (3:12)?

LAODICEA

14"And to the angel of the church in La-odice'a write: 'The words of
the Amen, the faithful and true witness, the beginning of God's creation.

[15]" 'I know your works: you are neither cold nor hot. Would that you were cold or hot! [16]So, because you are lukewarm, and neither cold nor hot, I will spew you out of my mouth. [17]For you say, I am rich, I have prospered, and I need nothing; not knowing that you are wretched, pitiable, poor, blind, and naked. [18]Therefore I counsel you to buy from me gold refined by fire, that you may be rich, and white garments to clothe you and to keep the shame of your nakedness from being seen, and salve to anoint your eyes, that you may see. [19]Those whom I love, I reprove and chasten; so be zealous and repent. [20]Behold, I stand at the door and knock; if any one hears my voice and opens the door, I will come in to him and eat with him, and he with me. [21]He who conquers, I will grant him to sit with me on my throne, as I myself conquered and sat down with my Father on his throne. [22]He who has an ear, let him hear what the Spirit says to the churches.' "

Laodicea was a city whose prosperity and self-sufficiency was well known throughout the ancient world. The city was devastated by an earthquake in the year A.D. 60 but rebuilt itself completely without any financial aid from Rome. Laodicea was a banking center but could also boast of a flourishing textile industry renowned for the clothing and carpeting manufactured from the soft, rich black wool produced in the region. Laodicea was also the home of a famous medical school, and its physicians were praised in ancient literature for discovering effective medicinal compounds including an eye salve made from oil and "Phrygian powder."

The church at Laodicea is reprimanded for being "neither cold nor hot" (3:15). Often this is taken to refer to a lukewarm religious fervor, its lack of zeal for the gospel. This interpretation is problematic, however, for it cannot fit the admonition: "Would that you were cold or hot! So, because you are lukewarm, and neither cold nor hot, I will spew you out of my mouth" (3:15–16). Why should the Lord of the church prefer Laodicea to be "cold" instead of "lukewarm"?

The best answer takes into consideration Laodicea's geographical situation, its medical tradition, and the Christian congregations in the Roman province of Phrygia. Laodicea's sister cities in Phrygia were Hierapolis, known for its medicinal hot-water springs, and Colossae, situated on the banks of the cold, pure waters of the Lycus River. Col. 4:13 tells us that Christian congregations existed in all three cities at the time of Paul. So when John of Patmos transmits the criticism that the church of Laodicea is neither cold nor hot, he is inviting a comparison with its two sister congregations in its immediate geographical area, an area with medicinal waters and a medical tradition.

The church at Laodicea had tried neutrality but in the process had lost its ability to heal. Neither cold nor hot, it could neither invigorate nor soothe. Casually blending into its environment, the congregation was a show church, wealthy and prosperous, on the surface in need of nothing (3:17). Such a condition had resulted, however, in a smugly self-satisfied church whose witness had become basically impotent. Such a church the risen Christ finds hard to swallow: he will spew it out of his mouth (3:16), and he describes it as poor, naked, and blind (3:17). The congregation is advised to turn now to Christ and to obtain from him the things that they think they already have, but do not: authentic richness tempered by testing, new garments to cover their shame, and medicine which can heal their blindness (3:18). Their impotent church is called to repent, for in their blind smugness they have locked Christ outside and he is still trying to get in (3:19–20).

So Christ comes to his church. He comes in Word and Sacrament (3:20). In fact, in the letter to the seven churches the coming of Christ to his churches is not yet his final coming at the end of time but his coming to each congregation to discover whether or not its witness in this world is an authentic one, faithful to the gospel. The one who walks among the lampstands visits his churches to make sure that he is actually present among them and that his presence is actualized in their inner life and proclamation.

Each church is representative of the whole church; each listens to what is said to the others. When John of Patmos, then, says *seven* churches, he means the whole church; he intends that his message be heard by all Christians of every time and place. For it is a revelation, a prophecy, a word from God.

"He who has an ear, let him hear what the Spirit says to the churches" (3:22).

4

The Liturgy of the Heavenly Court

REV. 4:1—5:14

4 After this I looked, and lo, in heaven an open door! And the first voice, which I had heard speaking to me like a trumpet, said, "Come up hither, and I will show you what must take place after this." ²At once I was in the Spirit, and lo, a throne stood in heaven, with one seated on the throne! ³And he who sat there appeared like jasper and carnelian, and round the throne was a rainbow that looked like an emerald. ⁴Round the throne were twenty-four thrones, and seated on the thrones were twenty-four elders, clad in white garments, with golden crowns upon their heads. ⁵From the throne issue flashes of lightning, and voices and peals of thunder, and before the throne burn seven torches of fire, which are the seven spirits of God; ⁶and before the throne there is as it were a sea of glass, like crystal.

And round the throne, on each side of the throne, are four living creatures, full of eyes in front and behind: ⁷the first living creature like a lion, the second living creature like an ox, the third living creature with the face of a man, and the fourth living creature like a flying eagle. ⁸And the four living creatures, each of them with six wings, are full of eyes all round and within, and day and night they never cease to sing,

"Holy, holy, holy, is the Lord God Almighty,
who was and is and is to come!"

⁹And whenever the living creatures give glory and honor and thanks to him who is seated on the throne, who lives for ever and ever, ¹⁰the twenty-four elders fall down before him who is seated on the throne and worship him who lives for ever and ever; they cast their crowns before the throne, singing,

¹¹"Worthy art thou, our Lord and God,
to receive glory and honor and power,
for thou didst create all things,
and by thy will they existed and were created."

5 And I saw in the right hand of him who was seated on the throne a

scroll written within and on the back, sealed with seven seals; [2]and I saw a strong angel proclaiming with a loud voice, "Who is worthy to open the scroll and break its seals?" [3]And no one in heaven or on earth or under the earth was able to open the scroll or to look into it, [4]and I wept much that no one was found worthy to open the scroll or to look into it. [5]Then one of the elders said to me, "Weep not; lo, the Lion of the tribe of Judah, the Root of David, has conquered, so that he can open the scroll and its seven seals."

[6]And between the throne and the four living creatures and among the elders, I saw a Lamb standing, as though it had been slain, with seven horns and with seven eyes, which are the seven spirits of God sent out into all the earth; [7]and he went and took the scroll from the right hand of him who was seated on the throne. [8]And when he had taken the scroll, the four living creatures and the twenty-four elders fell down before the Lamb, each holding a harp, and with golden bowls full of incense, which are the prayers of the saints; [9]and they sang a new song, saying,

"Worthy art thou to take the scroll and to open its seals,
for thou wast slain and by thy blood didst ransom men for God
from every tribe and tongue and people and nation,
[10]and hast made them a kingdom and priests to our God,
and they shall reign on earth."

[11]Then I looked, and I heard around the throne and the living creatures and the elders the voice of many angels, numbering myriads of myriads and thousands of thousands, [12]saying with a loud voice, "Worthy is the Lamb who was slain, to receive power and wealth and wisdom and might and honor and glory and blessing!" [13]And I heard every creature in heaven and on earth and under the earth and in the sea, and all therein, saying, "To him who sits upon the throne and to the Lamb be blessing and honor and glory and might for ever and ever!" [14]And the four living creatures said, "Amen!" and the elders fell down and worshiped.

The letter to the seven churches has been concluded, but what follows must not be detached from it. The author has purposely combined a number of elements to form the Book of Revelation, elements which include various pieces of literary material, a rich repertoire of symbols and images, and fusions of Old Testament texts and ideas. Out of this wealth of traditional elements John of Patmos has worked hard to produce a unitary composition, and he wants no one to subtract anything from it or add anything to it (22:18). He considers his work complete.

In the first three chapters he has challenged the churches to manifest the presence of Christ in a world hostile and threatening to them. He has described the internal conditions and the external pressures at work in the seven churches he knows, yet the conditions and pressures he describes have a familiar ring to Christians of every period in history. The symbols he chooses penetrate beyond their immediate reference points to mirror human situations in every age.

With Chapter 4, the major section of the Book of Revelation begins. Now that John has described his churches' situations and hostilities they face, he offers them his prophetic vision in order to help them understand why the world is hostile and threatening and in order to proclaim the good news of the future which God has in store for them. This section is dominated by the seven vision-cycles (6:1—21:5a), prefaced by the descriptions of the heavenly court (4:1—5:14) and followed by the description of the holy city of God (21:5b—22:5).

Chapter 4 opens with John seeing and hearing. The voice he hears at heaven's open door, a voice he has heard before (1:10), now invites him to begin where everything began, in the very presence of God (4:1-2). In familiar apocalyptic style John is invited to "come up" to see now what is future for those on earth, for before God the boundaries between past, present, and future are absent. John is called into the presence of the one "who is and who was and who is to come" (cf. 1:8; 4:8; 11:17). But one does not just walk in on heaven; one must first be "in the Spirit."

When John says "at once I was in the Spirit" (4:2), we must not too quickly judge the nature of this experience. We must not make of John a deranged fanatic the likes of which we would never trust today. If we wish to speak of John's vision of the heavenly throne room as an "ecstatic" experience, we should perhaps recall what the word "ecstasy" literally means, namely, "to get beyond oneself." Every human being has that possibility—to get beyond oneself. Every artist, every musician, every student reaches beyond what he or she alone is in order to create something new. Any experience of freedom from what we have been so far is an ecstatic experience.

John's reaching beyond himself and this world is also "in the Spirit." That means that his vision is theologically informed and

conditioned by the good news of God's presence, for the first
three chapters of Revelation have shown us that the work of "the
Spirit" happens within the community of God's people. As Paul
said in 1 Cor. 12:7, the gifts of the Spirit are given for the good of
the community, and one avails oneself of those gifts only as they
are given to the whole community. So when John of Patmos is
"in the Spirit," he is taken beyond himself to be united with the
people of God in their past, present, and future. "In the Spirit"
therefore does not refer to a simply subjective, individualistic
experience but to a communal one. For it is among the assembled people of God that the objective word is spoken and heard
(1:10; 2:7, 11, 17, 29; 3:6, 13, 22).

What John sees, then, is described in terms beyond himself,
theologically conditioned and shaped by the good news of God's
presence among his people. From within their language and
traditions John writes and is to be understood. The majestic sight
of the throne of God and the liturgy of the heavenly court reflect
the experiences of the people who have always been led by the
Spirit of God. And each symbol used in John's portrait is not to be
restricted to only one point of reference. Each symbol is purposely designed to recall a number of reference points from
within the life of John's community. The author writes "in the
Spirit," and he expects his readers to read "in the Spirit," that is,
from within the common heritage of God's people.

Therefore John's portrait of the throne of God reflects familiar
themes from the past. The jasper and carnelian (4:3) are among
the stones of paradise in Ezek. 28:13 and also represent the tribes
of Israel in Exod. 28:17-21. The rainbow around God's throne
recalls the promise to Noah that God's rule would be featured by
his mercy toward humankind. The twenty-four elders on
twenty-four thrones (4:4) reflect the ancient idea of the heavenly
council which is assembled to give counsel to God regarding
affairs in heaven and on earth (cf. Job 1-2 and Psalm 82). The
number twenty-four suggests the totality of God's people, a combination of twelve patriarchs and twelve apostles, now doing
priestly service (cf. 1 Chron. 24:4-5). The lightning and thunder
that proceed from God's throne (4:5) recall the many Old Testament passages that describe God's awesome power in terms of

the activity of nature (cf. Exod. 19:16ff.; Ps. 18:12ff.), and the menorah is symbolic of the fullness of God's presence.

The priestly service of the twenty-four elders is not to counsel but to praise. They lead all of creation, animate and inanimate (4:6–7), in praising the Creator. The four living creatures resembling a lion, an ox, a man, and an eagle eventually came to represent the four evangelists in Christian interpretation and art after the second century. For John they represent all living things, and they praise the Creator with an unceasing Sanctus: "Holy, holy, holy, is the Lord God Almighty, who was and is and is to come!" (4:8) And they are joined by the elders who address the Creator with the words:

> Worthy are thou, our Lord and God,
> to receive glory and honor and power,
> for thou didst create all things,
> and by thy will they existed and were created. (4:11)

Now John's attention focuses on a scroll held in God's right hand (5:1). The symbol of the scroll is that all of world history is subject to the will and power of God. But the scroll is sealed, and "no one in heaven or on earth or under the earth was able to open the scroll or to look into it" (5:3). No one is worthy to unravel the mystery of time and existence, of a hostile and fallen world and its future. No one, except "the Lion of the tribe of Judah," "the Root of David," "the Lamb who was slain" (5:5–6, 12).

These three titles come from the heritage of Jewish and Christian messianic theology and have a richness understood only by those who share that heritage. The first title is taken from the context of Jacob's final blessing of his sons in Gen. 49:9–10. Judah is called a "lion's whelp" and is told that the scepter shall not depart from him "until Shiloh come(s)" (KJV). In the Judaism of John's day this passage was interpreted as a reference to the coming of the Messiah. The second title, "the Root of David," recalls Isaiah's words: "There shall come forth a shoot from the stump of Jesse . . ." and "In that day the root of Jesse shall stand as an ensign to the peoples; him shall the nations seek . . ." (Isa. 11:1, 10). Both passages refer to Jesse, the father of David, and they look forward to the coming of the ideal king upon whom the

"Spirit of the Lord shall rest" (11:2). Isaiah's words were interpreted messianically in the Christian church as a reference to the
coming of Jesus (cf. Rom. 15:12).

The third title, "the Lamb who was slain," occurs twenty-eight
times in the Book of Revelation. John's combination of this title
with the titles "Lion of the tribe of Judah" and "Root of David"
indicate what kind of a messianic ruler Jesus came to be: his
cross is the sign of his victory and rule. This identifying combination is made elsewhere also, for example, in 17:14 where the
Lord of lords and King of kings is none other than the Lamb, and
in 19:11–16 where the same conqueror, leading the armies of
heaven, is clad in a robe dipped in (his own) blood.

The symbol "the Lamb who was slain" has various antece-
dents in Old Testament tradition, all of which figure in John's
use of it. It recalls the slaughtering of the passover lamb and
Israel's exodus from Egypt (cf. 1 Cor. 5:7; 1 Pet. 1:18–19). Isa.
53:7, "like a lamb that is led to the slaughter, and like a sheep
that before its shearers is dumb, so he opened not his mouth," is
applied to Jesus in Acts 8:32. The imagery of the conquering
lamb is also found in the apocalyptic tradition before John, for
example, in 1 Enoch 90. John's combination of imagery, however, leaves no doubt about the identity of the conqueror: Jesus
Christ crucified.

The reason for the Lamb's worthiness to open the scrolls is
given in the song of redemption in Rev. 5:9–10. The Lamb who
was slain has ransomed people for God from every nation and has
made them a kingdom and priests to God. The concept of the
sacrificial lamb recalls that the significance of a sacrifice is in the
declaration that more is owed to God than what we by ourselves
and by our own lives can offer. A sacrifice is a confession that we
have fallen short, not a claim that we have now caught up. But
the good news that John wants his audience to hear is that the
Lamb has caught us up, once and for all. By his cross Jesus has
ransomed us all, "every tribe and tongue and people and nation,"
and because of him the debts of our shortcomings no longer stand
against us. The effect of that act of ransoming us from our
shortcomings is that we are now "a kingdom and priests" to God,

that is, we are now set apart for God's special use in this world (cf. 1:5–6).

The Lamb who was slain is the only one worthy to open the scroll that is held in God's right hand (5:1). In other words, the cross of Christ is the means for interpreting our past, present, and future. Through Christ crucified we are able to understand the fallen, hostile world, and in him to see it redeemed (5:9–10).

So the hymn of creation in 4:11 is joined with the hymn of redemption in 5:9–10, and the liturgy of the heavenly court concludes with a stirring doxology:

Worthy is the Lamb who was slain, to receive power and wealth and wisdom and might and honor and glory and blessing! (5:12)

To him who sits upon the throne and to the Lamb be blessing and honor and glory and might for ever and ever! (5:13)

And all the people said "Amen!" (5:14).

5

The Four Horsemen

REV. 6:1–8

6 Now I saw when the Lamb opened one of the seven seals, and I heard one of the four living creatures say, as with a voice of thunder, "Come!" ²And I saw, and behold, a white horse, and its rider had a bow; and a crown was given to him, and he went out conquering and to conquer.

³When he opened the second seal, I heard the second living creature say, "Come!" ⁴And out came another horse, bright red; its rider was permitted to take peace from the earth, so that men should slay one another; and he was given a great sword.

⁵When he opened the third seal, I heard the third living creature say, "Come!" And I saw, and behold, a black horse, and its rider had a balance in his hand; ⁶and I heard what seemed to be a voice in the midst of the four living creatures saying, "A quart of wheat for a denarius, and three quarts of barley for a denarius; but do not harm oil and wine!"

⁷When he opened the fourth seal, I heard the voice of the fourth living creature say, "Come!" ⁸And I saw, and behold, a pale horse, and its rider's name was Death, and Hades followed him; and they were given power over a fourth of the earth, to kill with sword and with famine and with pestilence and by wild beasts of the earth.

The book of the seven seals resting in God's right hand (5:1) reminds us that the history of this world began and will end according to the will and power of the Creator. This world did not have its beginning by chance, nor will it come to its end by chance. It began not by human will, nor will it end by human will. The plan of God for the creation encompasses both its beginning and its end, and all of its history is subject to God's rule.

Yet that fact, comforting as it at first might sound, causes the most profound questioning about the very nature of God. If history unfolds under the power of God, why is there so much suf-

64

fering, so much evil, so much oppression in this world? What kind of God would allow the constant personal tragedy and corporate human disaster which people experience each day? It is a question which John's own churches are asking: "O Sovereign Lord, holy and true, how long before thou wilt judge and avenge our blood on those who dwell upon the earth?" (6:10).

For an answer John takes his readers into the very presence of God, into the heavenly throne room, where they hear another question: "Who is worthy to open the scroll and break its seals?" (5:2). In other words, who is able to resolve the deep questions of the history of this world and of our existence within it? At first no name is forthcoming, and John experiences some despair that the question might never have an answer (5:3–4)—until the silence is broken and a name is finally given: the Lamb who was slain, the Lion of the tribe of Judah, the Root of David (5:5–14).

This is no glib answer to just another question. We are immediately at the very heart of John's theology, applied now to the everyday situation of his readers. In his letters to the seven churches (2:1—3:22) John has recognized the external and internal pressures facing the churches, but he nevertheless places before each church the same challenge: is Christ present in your midst or absent from it? It is through his church that Christ's presence is to be realized in this world, and his presence—or his absence—will explain the perplexing situations of his people. In his presence disaster and death never have the last word.

That is the message of the book of the seven seals. The problems of world history and of human experience within it are not resolved until the creation is complete. And the creation is not complete until the lordship of Christ is lived within it. What is being offered here is not a periodization of world history into seven great epochs, but rather a means of interpreting our own life experience. This is seen in the opening of the first four seals when the four living creatures of 4:6–9, representing all living things, beckon John to witness what all creatures witness, portrayed in the vivid imagery of the four horsemen of the Apocalypse.

Once again, the symbolism used by John of Patmos is not simply his own, but it comes from the rich storehouse of the traditions of God's people, the community molded by the Spirit of God. The imagery of the four horsemen recalls Zechariah's visions of the variously colored horses sent out to patrol the earth (1:8–17; 6:1–8). But the four horsemen in Rev. 6:1–8 do more than patrol, and as John and the living creatures watch they bring disaster upon disaster.

The first rider represents military conquest, riding out with bow in hand and adorned with a crown. The color of his horse is white, the color of regal authority and power, and he goes out "conquering and to conquer." His objective is to subdue other nations and to place them under his rule.

The second rider's horse is red, the color of blood, and his sword is the kind used not in open warfare but in terrorist attacks and close confrontations. In contrast to the first rider the emphasis here is on less formal combat, on internal disorder such as assassinations, violent subversion from within, or simply the horror that human beings take the lives of other human beings (6:4).

The third rider is on a black horse and holds a balance in his hand. The scene is one of famine, when a day's wages buy only the bare necessities for subsistence living (6:6). But restraints are placed on this rider: "A quart of wheat for a denarius, and three quarts of barley for a denarius; but do not harm oil and wine!" (6:6). The voice is God's, coming from the midst of the four living creatures who stand on each side of the throne (4:6), the throne encircled by the rainbow (4:3). Famine will not have the last word.

The fourth rider has a name. His name is Death. He rides a pale horse and is accompanied by Hades, the ancient god of the underworld and a symbol for the abode of the dead. The objective of this horseman and his grotesque companion is that of utter destruction, the ultimate doom from which there is no return. They represent a heightened finality to the work of the first three horsemen, the methods of death reminiscent of the "four sore acts of judgment" in Ezek. 14:21: sword, famine, evil beasts, and pestilence. Even here, however, limitations are placed on this dreaded pair: their power over the earth is by no means complete (Rev. 6:8). For we already know who has the keys to Death and Hades (1:18).

The four horsemen of the Apocalypse represent the full scale of personal and corporate disasters experienced in every period of human history. The book of the seven seals is therefore not a linear chronology of the history of the world, but rather it is a statement that such disasters will not overcome God's people. The power of each disaster is *given*, and the destructive use of that power is limited. Furthermore, what is still to come in the opening of the last three seals is written in order to make sense of life in a hostile and turbulent world.

6

The Book of the
Seven Seals

REV. 6:9—7:17

⁹When he opened the fifth seal, I saw under the altar the souls of those who had been slain for the word of God and for the witness they had borne; ¹⁰they cried out with a loud voice, "O Sovereign Lord, holy and true, how long before thou wilt judge and avenge our blood on those who dwell upon the earth?" ¹¹Then they were each given a white robe and told to rest a little longer, until the number of their fellow servants and their brethren should be complete, who were to be killed as they themselves had been.

¹²When he opened the sixth seal, I looked, and behold, there was a great earthquake; and the sun became black as sackcloth, the full moon became like blood, ¹³and the stars of the sky fell to the earth as the fig tree sheds its winter fruit when shaken by a gale; ¹⁴the sky vanished like a scroll that is rolled up, and every mountain and island was removed from its place. ¹⁵Then the kings of the earth and the great men and the generals and the rich and the strong, and every one, slave and free, hid in the caves and among the rocks of the mountains, ¹⁶calling to the mountains and rocks, "Fall on us and hide us from the face of him who is seated on the throne, and from the wrath of the Lamb; ¹⁷for the great day of their wrath has come, and who can stand before it?"

7 After this I saw four angels standing at the four corners of the earth, holding back the four winds of the earth, that no wind might blow on earth or sea or against any tree. ²Then I saw another angel ascend from the rising of the sun, with the seal of the living God, and he called with a loud voice to the four angels who had been given power to harm earth and sea, ³saying, "Do not harm the earth or the sea or the trees, till we have sealed the servants of our God upon their foreheads." ⁴And I heard the number of the sealed, a hundred and forty-four thousand sealed, out of every tribe of the sons of Israel, ⁵twelve thousand sealed out of the tribe of Judah, twelve thousand of the tribe of Reuben, twelve thousand of the tribe of Gad, ⁶twelve thousand of the tribe of Asher, twelve

68

thousand of the tribe of Naph'tali, twelve thousand of the tribe of Man-
as'seh, [7]twelve thousand of the tribe of Simeon, twelve thousand of the
tribe of Levi, twelve thousand of the tribe of Is'sachar, [8]twelve thousand
of the tribe of Zeb'ulun, twelve thousand of the tribe of Joseph, twelve
thousand sealed out of the tribe of Benjamin.

[9]After this I looked, and behold, a great multitude which no man could
number, from every nation, from all tribes and peoples and tongues,
standing before the throne and before the Lamb, clothed in white robes,
with palm branches in their hands, [10]and crying out with a loud voice,
"Salvation belongs to our God who sits upon the throne, and to the
Lamb!" [11]And all the angels stood round the throne and round the elders
and the four living creatures, and they fell on their faces before the
throne and worshiped God, [12]saying, "Amen! Blessing and glory and
wisdom and thanksgiving and honor and power and might be to our God
for ever and ever! Amen."

[13]Then one of the elders addressed me, saying, "Who are these,
clothed in white robes, and whence have they come?" [14]I said to him,
"Sir, you know." And he said to me, "These are they who have come out
of the great tribulation; they have washed their robes and made them
white in the blood of the Lamb.

[15]Therefore are they before the throne of God,
    and serve him day and night within his temple;
    and he who sits upon the throne will shelter them with his presence.
[16]They shall hunger no more, neither thirst any more;
    the sun shall not strike them, nor any scorching heat.
[17]For the Lamb in the midst of the throne will be their shepherd,
    and he will guide them to springs of living water;
and God will wipe away every tear from their eyes."

In the Introduction we spoke of the series of word pictures in the
Book of Revelation organized around the number seven. The
letter to the seven churches is followed by seven vision-cycles
depicting the book of the seven seals, the seven trumpets, the
seven visions of conflict, the seven visions of Mount Zion, the
seven bowls of the wrath of God, the seven visions of the fall of
"Babylon," and the seven visions of recompense. Beginning
with the book of the seven seals, the seventh number in each
series sets in motion the unfolding of the next septet, connecting
each series and creating a sense of anticipation for what is to
come.

The book of the seven seals represents the history of human experience in this world. The book is held in the right hand of the Creator (5:1) as a sign that God has not abdicated his rule over this world, in spite of the terrors at work within it. These terrors are depicted as the first four seals are opened, with the emergence of the four horsemen portraying military conquest, internal violence, famine, and death. The power of each, however, is limited; the power of each is a derived power. The message of the book of the seven seals is a message of promise: the personal and corporate disasters experienced in this world do not spell the end for God's people. The terrors will not have the last word. There is more to come.

However, to allow the matter to rest with the disasters which always threaten humanity would be offering a far too general word. Therefore the opening of the fifth seal gives a specific word to John's readers in terms of their own particular situation. The terror which they face is that of official persecution by the Roman government. They have been oppressed on account of the Word of God and the witness they have given (6:9; cf. 1:9). With the opening of the fifth seal John sees the martyrs and hears their cry: "O Sovereign Lord, holy and true, how long before thou wilt judge and avenge our blood on those who dwell upon earth?" (6:10).

This desperate cry might strike us as somewhat offensive, especially if we view it as a bitter cry for revenge. In the Old Testament, however, the request that God avenge the righteous sufferer is primarily an act of faith, a steadfast clinging to *the power of God* in the face of oppression. It also reflects a concern for God's reputation in the world rather than a concern for personal revenge (cf. Pss. 42:9–10; 79:10; 94:1–3). The martyrs' cry also recognizes that their vindication is in the hands of God, to be accomplished when and how he wills.

Both the martyrs' question and the answer to it reveal the corporate dimension of the oppression. The Word of God and the witness which his people bear have social and political consequences. The message of the gospel is a confrontation with the world and its values, and when that message is preached and lived, the worldly powers simply do not roll over and die. They may try to co-opt it, to outbluff it, to stamp it out, and eventually to silence those who proclaim it. Witness to the lordship of Christ will necessarily result in anxiety and hostility among those who desire to exercise their own lordship in this world. Their oppressive reaction is proof that the gospel is being heard. But when some of God's people are silenced, others will arise until God declares their number to be complete (6:11). The solidarity of his oppressed people is a gift to them from God, a gift by which they learn that they are not alone. And they have a future, for they are told "to rest a little longer" (6:11).

The opening of the sixth seal depicts the heightened anxiety of the worldly powers as they see their power slipping out of their hands (6:15). The function of natural calamity is to remind human beings of the limitations of their power, that they do not have ultimate control over their lives. In the Old Testament great cosmic disturbances are a sign of God's power and visitation, designed to shatter the self-sufficiency of those who rely only on themselves (cf. Exod. 19:18; Joel 2:31; Isa. 2:17–19; 13:9–10). But not everyone learns this lesson. Those who have sought their security only in this world will experience shock and anxiety at the breakdown of the natural order even while they still foolishly seek refuge in this world (6:16).

Therefore with the calamities of nature a lesson is to be learned about human existence *now*. Such calamities are not to promote speculation about the future, about the time of the end of all things. In Chapter 7, John tells us that the destruction of all things is delayed until the assembling of God's people is complete. The present time is the time of God's patience, the time of his restraining the winds of destruction, the time of the gathering of his people (7:1–3).

Two pictures are presented which describe the people of God: the 144,000 sealed (7:4–8) and the countless multitude (7:9–17). The first picture affirms the continuity of the Christian church with Israel. The number twelve functions as a symbol of completeness, and 12,000 times twelve refers to the fullness of the Israel of God. Once again, the symbol of the seal marking the foreheads of God's servants (7:3ff.) is not to be limited to only one reference point: it functions as an identity mark for God's

people, from the Exodus blood mark to Christian baptism, from
the protective mark of Ezek. 9:4 to the marks of Christian suffering in Gal. 6:17. This is a new creation, this Israel of God, of
which Paul speaks in Gal. 6:15–16. Neither cosmic calamities nor
the forces of evil nor the final destruction at the end of time will
overwhelm those whose identity and security are found within
the Israel of God.

The second picture of God's Israel shows that the number
12,000 in the previous picture is symbolic, for John sees a "multitude which no man could number" joining with the heavenly
court in its liturgy of praise (7:9–17). The Israel of God is now
defined: it includes people "from every nation, from all tribes
and peoples and tongues" (7:9). Their identity is further explained: they wear white robes, robes which have been made
white by the cross of Christ (7:14). They have come out of "the
great tribulation," that time of testing for which John is preparing
his readers (cf. 3:10). What has given them their white robes is
not their achievement during the time of testing. Rather, their
apparel of victory is theirs because of the death of their Lord. As
God provided for the returning exiles of old (Isa. 49:10), their
Lord will provide for them eternally (7:15–17).

But for John's readers this promise is yet to be fulfilled. The
seventh seal is yet to be opened. And with the opening of the last
seal comes the announcement of the lordship of Christ (11:15–
19). That lordship is not simply a natural development within
human history, but the decisive interruption of the forces attempting to hold sway in this world. As the seventh seal is
opened, a dramatic silence occurs, for what follows is decisive.
So that there is no mistake about it, the opening of the seventh
seal sets in motion the seven angelic trumpets before the throne
of God.

7

The Seven Trumpets

REV. 8:1—9:21

8 When the Lamb opened the seventh seal, there was silence in heaven for about half an hour. ²Then I saw the seven angels who stand before God, and seven trumpets were given to them. ³And another angel came and stood at the altar with a golden censer; and he was given much incense to mingle with the prayers of all the saints upon the golden altar before the throne; ⁴and the smoke of the incense rose with the prayers of the saints from the hand of the angel before God. ⁵Then the angel took the censer and filled it with fire from the altar and threw it on the earth; and there were peals of thunder, loud noises, flashes of lightning, and an earthquake.

⁶Now the seven angels who had the seven trumpets made ready to blow them.

⁷The first angel blew his trumpet, and there followed hail and fire, mixed with blood, which fell on the earth; and a third of the earth was burnt up, and a third of the trees were burnt up, and all green grass was burnt up.

⁸The second angel blew his trumpet, and something like a great mountain, burning with fire, was thrown into the sea; ⁹and a third of the sea became blood, a third of the living creatures in the sea died, and a third of the ships were destroyed.

¹⁰The third angel blew his trumpet, and a great star fell from heaven, blazing like a torch, and it fell on a third of the rivers and on the fountains of water. ¹¹The name of the star is Wormwood. A third of the waters became wormwood, and many men died of the water, because it was made bitter.

¹²The fourth angel blew his trumpet, and a third of the sun was struck, and a third of the moon, and a third of the stars, so that a third of their light was darkened; a third of the day was kept from shining, and likewise a third of the night.

¹³Then I looked, and I heard an eagle crying with a loud voice, as it

flew in midheaven, "Woe, woe, woe to those who dwell on the earth, at the blasts of the other trumpets which the three angels are about to blow!"

9 And the fifth angel blew his trumpet, and I saw a star fallen from heaven to earth, and he was given the key of the shaft of the bottomless pit; [2]he opened the shaft of the bottomless pit, and from the shaft rose smoke like the smoke of a great furnace, and the sun and the air were darkened with the smoke from the shaft. [3]Then from the smoke came locusts on the earth, and they were given power like the power of scorpions of the earth; [4]they were told not to harm the grass of the earth or any green growth or any tree, but only those of mankind who have not the seal of God upon their foreheads; [5]they were allowed to torture them for five months, but not to kill them, and their torture was like the torture of a scorpion, when it stings a man. [6]And in those days men will seek death and will not find it; they will long to die, and death will fly from them.

[7]In appearance the locusts were like horses arrayed for battle; on their heads were what looked like crowns of gold; their faces were like human faces, [8]their hair like women's hair, and their teeth like lions' teeth; [9]they had scales like iron breastplates, and the noise of their wings was like the noise of many chariots with horses rushing into battle. [10]They have tails like scorpions, and stings, and their power of hurting men for five months lies in their tails. [11]They have as king over them the angel of the bottomless pit; his name in Hebrew is Abad'don and in Greek he is called Apol'lyon.

[12]The first woe has passed; behold, two woes are still to come.

[13]Then the sixth angel blew his trumpet, and I heard a voice from the four horns of the golden altar before God, [14]saying to the sixth angel who had the trumpet, "Release the four angels who are bound at the great river Eu-phra'tes." [15]So the four angels were released, who had been held ready for the hour, the day, the month, and the year, to kill a third of mankind. [16]The number of the troops of cavalry was twice ten thousand times ten thousand; I heard their number. [17]And this was how I saw the horses in my vision: the riders wore breastplates the color of fire and of sapphire and of sulphur, and the heads of the horses were like lions' heads, and fire and smoke and sulphur issued from their mouths. [18]By these three plagues a third of mankind was killed, by the fire and smoke and sulphur issuing from their mouths. [19]For the power of the horses is in their mouths and in their tails; their tails are like serpents, with heads, and by means of them they wound.

[20]The rest of mankind, who were not killed by these plagues, did not

repent of the works of their hands nor give up worshiping demons and idols of gold and silver and bronze and stone and wood, which cannot either see or hear or walk; [21]nor did they repent of their murders or their sorceries or their immorality or their thefts.

"When the Lamb opened the seventh seal, there was silence in heaven for about half an hour" (8:1). All the shouting, all the previous tumult dies. With the first six seals we have seen what the absence of Christ's lordship among humanity has meant: war and sedition, famine and death, the oppression of God's people by the desperate managers of the earth who are unable to face their own ultimate lack of power, who are unable to deal with their own death. Now with the opening of the seventh seal and the advent of the lordship of Christ, something new is introduced. Therefore the silence, as prophets often said: "Be silent before the Lord God! For the day of the Lord is at hand" (Zeph. 1:7; cf. Zech. 2:13; Hab. 2:20).

It is the opening of the seventh seal which signals the lordship of Christ, a picture which proclaims that the history of this world is incomplete without the incarnation. The Word was made flesh and dwelt among us, and that good news is the means by which Christ's presence continues to be manifest, wherever two or three are gathered, in water and Word, bread and wine. This is always something new, not simply a natural development within this world but a gift from beyond it. Therefore the silence, as psalmists often say:

> Let all mortal flesh keep silence,
> And with fear and trembling stand;
> Ponder nothing earthly minded,
> For with blessing in his hand,
> Christ, our God, to earth descendeth
> Our full homage to demand.
> (From the "Liturgy of St. James")

Once again, it is the setting of worship which provides the imagery which follows (8:2–5). Trumpets are used to gather God's people together to celebrate the great festivals (Num. 10:3, 10; 29:1). From ancient times the beautiful symbol of incense has portrayed the prayers of the people at worship ascending as a

fragrance pleasant and acceptable to God. John has already identified the incense with the prayers of the saints (5:8), and now the
trumpets herald God's response, for they announce the beginning of the reign of the new king (cf. 1 Kings 1:34, 39; 2 Kings
9:13). So when the seventh seal is opened and the lordship of
Christ is begun, the seven trumpets must make ready to sound.

Now John sees another angel who "was given much incense to
mingle with the prayers of all the saints" (8:3), and it is this angel
who *presents* his own incense along with the prayers of the saints
(8:4). One cannot help but wonder whether John has read the
letter to the Hebrews which speaks of Jesus as our high priest
before God, who "in the days of his flesh . . . offered up prayers
and supplications" (5:7), and who finally, having offered himself, now intercedes for us before the throne of God (4:14–16).
Eph. 5:2 speaks of the Christ who "loved us and gave himself up
for us, a fragrant offering and sacrifice to God." If John is writing
with these ideas in mind then the identity of the angel in Rev.
8:3–5 is clear. It is a picture of Christ himself.

The trumpets begin to peal when this angel fills the censer
with fire from the altar and casts it upon the earth. This is not
only an action of judgment but also one of purification. It recalls
the action of the angel in Isaiah's inaugural vision, taking burning coal from the altar and touching Isaiah's lips (Isa. 6:6–7). But
purification means at the same time judgment, and Isaiah recognizes this: "Woe is me! For I am lost; for I am a man of unclean
lips, and I dwell in the midst of a people of unclean lips" (6:5).
But purification does not mean Isaiah's destruction; instead it is
good news, for the angel says "Behold, this (coal) has touched
your lips; your guilt is taken away, and your sin forgiven" (6:7).

Purification does not come easy. Hot coal burns, as does the
cauterization of an infected wound. Surgery might take away a
part of us in order to make us well; we may not want to lose
anything, but pain and loss may be necessary in order for us to
experience actual healing. The lordship of Christ can be a reality
only when we are ready to give up some of the things which we
hold so dear in this world, especially if we have become so at-
tached to this world that our lives have become determined by it.

When our new king, Christ our Lord, begins his reign there

will be a confrontation with the world, its values, and its power. A process of purification begins as the refiner's fire is cast toward the earth (8:5). One after another the trumpets sound, and no part of the earth remains unaffected: the food that we eat (8:7–8), the water that we drink (8:10–11), the sun and moon and stars that light our days and nights (8:12). The power of each is assailed so that we do not make any one of them our god. But the good news is that Christ reigns and that his future is offered to those whose lives are determined by him.

There are some who will not receive that good news but would rather attempt to secure their own future out of their own resources. Above them the vulture flies, for he knows their lot is nothing but woe (8:13).* The bird of prey waits for ruin as the trumpets continue to sound and the refining becomes more intense. The fifth trumpet signals the release of a horde of locusts from the "bottomless pit," an image used throughout Revelation for the reservoir of all evil. This plague of locusts, the biblical symbol for destruction (cf. Deut. 28:42; Ps. 78:46), afflicts all those "who have not the seal of God upon their foreheads" (9:4). The locusts are given a scorpionlike power, and their poisonous strike inflicts such torment that its victims desire death but do not receive it. The king of the locusts is called "Abaddon" in Hebrew and "Apollyon" in Greek (9:11). These two names, along with "Wormwood" in 8:11, are symbolic code words to be understood within the framework of the tradition and experience of John's readers.

In a third stage of the fourfold purging of the earth signaled by the first four trumpets (8:2–12), the star called "Wormwood" falls into the earth's water supply to make it bitter, the reverse of the miracle at Marah where bitter water became sweet when Moses cast a tree into it (Exod. 15:25). Jewish Christians would recognize the Hebrew word "Abaddon" as an allusion to the ruler of the underworld, the abyss, the "bottomless pit" (Rev. 9:11), al-

---

*Notice in 8:13 that the King James Version proposes the word "angel" for the word translated "eagle" in the Revised Standard Version. The former is based on lesser manuscript evidence than is the latter. The Greek word for "eagle" can also mean "vulture" as in Luke 17:37. Other ancient Greek authors classified the vulture among the eagles.

ready personified in Job 28:22. Greek Christians would recognize "Apollyon" as a word meaning "Destroyer" and as a cryptic reference to the Greek god Apollo, whose symbol was the locust and whose name the Emperor Domitian, the persecutor of the church, used of himself.

The message of the vision of the seven trumpets is that those who insist on allowing their lives to be determined by this world will find no refuge within it, and yet they learn nothing from the disasters which come their way. Repentance is not on their agenda (9:20–21). Nor is the hymn of victory sung by the saints on their lips: "The kingdom of the world has become the kingdom of our Lord and of his Christ, and he shall reign for ever and ever" (11:15).

8

Prophet and
Witness

REV. 10:1—11:19

10 Then I saw another mighty angel coming down from heaven, wrapped in a cloud, with a rainbow over his head, and his face was like the sun, and his legs like pillars of fire. [2]He had a little scroll open in his hand. And he set his right foot on the sea, and his left foot on the land, [3]and called out with a loud voice, like a lion roaring; when he called out, the seven thunders sounded. [4]And when the seven thunders had sounded, I was about to write, but I heard a voice from heaven saying, "Seal up what the seven thunders have said, and do not write it down." [5]And the angel whom I saw standing on sea and land lifted up his right hand to heaven [6]and swore by him who lives for ever and ever, who created heaven and what is in it, the earth and what is in it, and the sea and what is in it, that there should be no more delay, [7]but that in the days of the trumpet call to be sounded by the seventh angel, the mystery of God, as he announced to his servants the prophets, should be fulfilled.

[8]Then the voice which I had heard from heaven spoke to me again, saying, "Go, take the scroll which is open in the hand of the angel who is standing on the sea and on the land." [9]So I went to the angel and told him to give me the little scroll; and he said to me, "Take it and eat; it will be bitter to your stomach, but sweet as honey in your mouth." [10]And I took the little scroll from the hand of the angel and ate it; it was sweet as honey in my mouth, but when I had eaten it my stomach was made bitter. [11]And I was told, "You must again prophesy about many peoples and nations and tongues and kings."

11 Then I was given a measuring rod like a staff, and I was told: "Rise and measure the temple of God and the altar and those who worship there, [2]but do not measure the court outside the temple; leave that out, for it is given over to the nations, and they will trample over the holy city for forty-two months. [3]And I will grant my two witnesses power to prophesy for one thousand two hundred and sixty days, clothed in sackcloth."

[4]These are the two olive trees and the two lampstands which stand before the Lord of the earth. [5]And if any one would harm them, fire pours from their mouth and consumes their foes; if any one would harm them, thus he is doomed to be killed. [6]They have power to shut the sky, that no rain may fall during the days of their prophesying, and they have power over the waters to turn them into blood, and to smite the earth with every plague, as often as they desire. [7]And when they have finished their testimony, the beast that ascends from the bottomless pit will make war upon them and conquer them and kill them, [8]and their dead bodies will lie in the street of the great city which is allegorically called Sodom and Egypt, where their Lord was crucified. [9]For three days and a half men from the peoples and tribes and tongues and nations gaze at their dead bodies and refuse to let them be placed in a tomb, [10]and those who dwell on the earth will rejoice over them and make merry and exchange presents, because these two prophets had been a torment to those who dwell on the earth. [11]But after the three and a half days a breath of life from God entered them, and they stood up on their feet, and great fear fell on those who saw them. [12]Then they heard a loud voice from heaven saying to them, "Come up hither!" And in the sight of their foes they went up to heaven in a cloud. [13]And at that hour there was a great earthquake, and a tenth of the city fell; seven thousand people were killed in the earthquake, and the rest were terrified and gave glory to the God of heaven.

[14]The second woe has passed; behold, the third woe is soon to come.

[15]Then the seventh angel blew his trumpet, and there were loud voices in heaven, saying, "The kingdom of the world has become the kingdom of our Lord and of his Christ, and he shall reign for ever and ever." [16]And the twenty-four elders who sit on their thrones before God fell on their faces and worshiped God, [17]saying,

"We give thanks to thee, Lord God Almighty, who art and who wast,
    that thou has taken thy great power and begun to reign.
[18]The nations raged, but thy wrath came,
    and the time for the dead to be judged,
for rewarding thy servants, the prophets and saints,
    and those who fear thy name, both small and great,
and for destroying the destroyers of the earth."

[19]Then God's temple in heaven was opened, and the ark of his covenant was seen within his temple; and there were flashes of lightning, loud noises, peals of thunder, an earthquake, and heavy hail.

The use of such symbols as "Wormwood," "Abaddon," and

"Apollyon" sheds light on John's own understanding of himself as a Christian prophet, that is, as a proclaimer of God's Word in the world. He knows the situation of his readers, and he offers them a message of encouragement and hope. Yet he will not engage in pandering, in telling them only what they would like to hear, in removing one edge of the gospel (cf. 1:16). The stumbling block of the cross is a stumbling block, a message of confrontation to those who would seek refuge in the powers of this world. For all its present force and glitter, Domitian's power is limited. The days of the hideous locust and his horde are numbered (9:4, 11).

The word of the prophet is also a word of explanation. It explains why the people of God are subject to the horrors and disasters that they face in this world. Because this world is a fallen world, in bondage to decay (cf. Rom. 8:21), the signs of decay are all around us: war, sedition, famine, and death. In the face of this the gospel gives us a point of reference from beyond this world from which we live our lives: in Christ God is for us and has provided for us beyond every disaster, even beyond death. In this gospel we are given a perspective from which we can evaluate our world, its standards, and its goals. The apocalyptic expression of the gospel emphasizes that those who take refuge in the values of this world are bound to its decay and have no means to enjoy the freedom of God's future. But that is to say that in the midst of decay there is hope: in the message of the gospel we have the means to enjoy the freedom of God's future *now*.

Those who proclaim this message, however, must realize that it is a bittersweet task (10:8–11). John reminds us of the commissioning of the prophet Ezekiel, who is told to open his mouth and eat what is given him (Ezek. 2:8—3:3). The scroll he is given represents the Word of God, and when Ezekiel consumes it he experiences a taste as sweet as honey in his mouth. "How sweet are thy words to my taste," the psalmist had said, "sweeter than honey to my mouth!" (Ps. 119:103). So for John the gospel is a message that is given to us, not of our own creating (Rev. 10:8–9). When we first hear it we experience the sweetness of its message of freedom and hope. But when it gets beyond our palate, when

we start digesting it, this same message may not be so sweet
(10:10). For the gospel challenges our values and our attachment
to this world and calls us to live from a perspective beyond this
world.

That does not mean a flight from this world but a confrontation
with it. The prophet of God is not to be locked up in his or her
study nor to be thought of as an institutional prisoner doing
"church work." The pastor is not a "hired hand" doing the bidding of the church council nor a bought voice expected to pander
to the cultural or religious politics of the moment. Lay person or
clergy, the prophet of God is called to prophesy "about many
peoples and nations and tongues and kings" (10:11). The prophet
of God is called also to "measure the temple of God and the altar
and those who worship there" (11:1).

Such measuring is another image of hope. It recalls the
measuring of the temple in Ezekiel 40—42, a picture signifying
the careful restoration of God's house according to his standards.
But it is also a challenge to us, to make sure that our church
points beyond itself to the good news of God for which it stands.
The measuring of the church, its worship, and those who gather
there is a constant task and serves to remind us that we do not
place our confidence in buildings, in liturgies, or in numbers but
in the Word of Christ crucified and risen.

The prophets who are witnesses are also measured. Even
though it seems that 11:5-6 speak of the power of the prophetic
witnesses themselves, they actually tell us that the witnesses are
measured by the highest standards possible. The witnesses must
meet the standards of an Elijah, whose ministry was to announce
the power of God in fire (2 Kings 1:10ff.) and drought (1 Kings
17:1ff.). They must meet the standards of a Moses, whose ministry was to announce the plagues which befell the earth (Exodus
7—12). The standards of Elijah and Moses remind today's
prophetic witnesses that their power rests not in their own word,
their own persons, or their own popularity, but in the Word of
God which they are *given* to proclaim.

The message of God's prophets, then, is a bittersweet one. It is
the message of God's own witnesses which calls into question
the values and standards of this world and confronts "those who

dwell on the earth" (11:10). The phrase "those who dwell on the
earth" is a phrase used often by John to designate particularly
those who take refuge in this world and who choose to live solely
out of their own resources. They will be found both outside and
inside the church, and they will not take kindly to the message of
God's prophets and witnesses. The fate of God's prophetic witnesses may turn out to be that of their Lord (11:8), but so also will
be their future (11:9–11), for their future is God's future. For
them Christ reigns *now*, and therefore their future is secure
(11:15–19).

9

The Church's Conflict with the Worldly Powers

REV. 12:1—14:20

12 And a great portent appeared in heaven, a woman clothed with the sun, with the moon under her feet, and on her head a crown of twelve stars; ²she was with child and she cried out in her pangs of birth, in anguish for delivery. ³And another portent appeared in heaven; behold, a great red dragon, with seven heads and ten horns, and seven diadems upon his heads. ⁴His tail swept down a third of the stars of heaven, and cast them to the earth. And the dragon stood before the woman who was about to bear a child, that he might devour her child when she brought it forth; ⁵she brought forth a male child, one who is to rule all the nations with a rod of iron, but her child was caught up to God and to his throne, ⁶and the woman fled into the wilderness, where she has a place prepared by God, in which to be nourished for one thousand two hundred and sixty days.

⁷Now war arose in heaven, Michael and his angels fighting against the dragon; and the dragon and his angels fought, ⁸but they were defeated and there was no longer any place for them in heaven. ⁹And the great dragon was thrown down, that ancient serpent, who is called the Devil and Satan, the deceiver of the whole world—he was thrown down to the earth, and his angels were thrown down with him. ¹⁰And I heard a loud voice in heaven, saying, "Now the salvation and the power and the kingdom of our God and the authority of his Christ have come, for the accuser of our brethren has been thrown down, who accuses them day and night before our God. ¹¹And they have conquered him by the blood of the Lamb and by the word of their testimony, for they loved not their lives even unto death. ¹²Rejoice then, O heaven and you that dwell therein! But woe to you, O earth and sea, for the devil has come down to you in great wrath, because he knows that his time is short!"

¹³And when the dragon saw that he had been thrown down to the earth, he pursued the woman who had borne the male child. ¹⁴But the woman was given the two wings of the great eagle that she might fly

from the serpent into the wilderness, to the place where she is to be nourished for a time, and times, and half a time. [15]The serpent poured water like a river out of his mouth after the woman, to sweep her away with the flood. [16]But the earth came to the help of the woman, and the earth opened its mouth and swallowed the river which the dragon had poured from his mouth. [17]Then the dragon was angry with the woman, and went off to make war on the rest of her offspring, on those who keep the commandments of God and bear testimony to Jesus. And he stood on the sand of the sea.

13 And I saw a beast rising out of the sea, with ten horns and seven heads, with ten diadems upon its horns and a blasphemous name upon its heads. [2]And the beast that I saw was like a leopard, its feet were like a bear's, and its mouth was like a lion's mouth. And to it the dragon gave his power and his throne and great authority. [3]One of its heads seemed to have a mortal wound, but its mortal wound was healed, and the whole earth followed the beast with wonder. [4]Men worshiped the dragon, for he had given his authority to the beast, and they worshiped the beast, saying, "Who is like the beast, and who can fight against it?"

[5]And the beast was given a mouth uttering haughty and blasphemous words, and it was allowed to exercise authority for forty-two months; [6]it opened its mouth to utter blasphemies against God, blaspheming his name and his dwelling, that is, those who dwell in heaven. [7]Also it was allowed to make war on the saints and to conquer them. And authority was given it over every tribe and people and tongue and nation, [8]and all who dwell on earth will worship it, every one whose name has not been written before the foundation of the world in the book of life of the Lamb that was slain. [9]If any one has an ear, let him hear:

[10]If any one is to be taken captive,
    to captivity he goes;
if any one slays with the sword,
    with the sword must he be slain.

Here is a call for the endurance and faith of the saints.

[11]Then I saw another beast which rose out of the earth; it had two horns like a lamb and it spoke like a dragon. [12]It exercises all the authority of the first beast in its presence, and makes the earth and its inhabitants worship the first beast, whose mortal wound was healed. [13]It works great signs, even making fire come down from heaven to earth in the sight of men; [14]and by the signs which it is allowed to work in the presence of the beast, it deceives those who dwell on earth, bidding them make an image for the beast which was wounded by the sword and yet lived; [15]and it was allowed to give breath to the image of the beast so

that the image of the beast should even speak, and to cause those who would not worship the image of the beast to be slain. [16]Also it causes all, both small and great, both rich and poor, both free and slave, to be marked on the right hand or the forehead, [17]so that no one can buy or sell unless he has the mark, that is, the name of the beast or the number of its name. [18]This calls for wisdom: let him who has understanding reckon the number of the beast, for it is a human number, its number is six hundred and sixty-six.

14 Then I looked, and lo, on Mount Zion stood the Lamb, and with him a hundred and forty-four thousand who had his name and his Father's name written on their foreheads. [2]And I heard a voice from heaven like the sound of many waters and like the sound of loud thunder; the voice I heard was like the sound of harpers playing on their harps, [3]and they sing a new song before the throne and before the four living creatures and before the elders. No one could learn that song except the hundred and forty-four thousand who had been redeemed from the earth. [4]It is these who have not defiled themselves with women, for they are chaste; it is these who follow the Lamb wherever he goes; these have been redeemed from mankind as first fruits for God and the Lamb, [5]and in their mouth no lie was found, for they are spotless.

[6]Then I saw another angel flying in midheaven, with an eternal gospel to proclaim to those who dwell on earth, to every nation and tribe and tongue and people; [7]and he said with a loud voice, "Fear God and give him glory, for the hour of his judgment has come; and worship him who made heaven and earth, the sea and the fountains of water."

[8]Another angel, a second, followed, saying, "Fallen, fallen is Babylon the great, she who made all nations drink the wine of her impure passion."

[9]And another angel, a third, followed them, saying with a loud voice, "If any one worships the beast and its image, and receives a mark on his forehead or on his hand, [10]he also shall drink the wine of God's wrath, poured unmixed into the cup of his anger, and he shall be tormented with fire and brimstone in the presence of the holy angels and in the presence of the Lamb. [11]And the smoke of their torment goes up for ever and ever; and they have no rest, day or night, these worshipers of the beast and its image, and whoever receives the mark of its name."

[12]Here is a call for the endurance of the saints, those who keep the commandments of God and the faith of Jesus.

[13]And I heard a voice from heaven saying, "Write this: Blessed are the dead who die in the Lord henceforth." "Blessed indeed," says the Spirit, "that they may rest from their labors, for their deeds follow them!"

[14]Then I looked, and lo, a white cloud, and seated on the cloud one like a son of man, with a golden crown on his head, and a sharp sickle in his hand. [15]And another angel came out of the temple, calling with a loud voice to him who sat upon the cloud, "Put in your sickle, and reap, for the hour to reap has come, for the harvest of the earth is fully ripe." [16]So he who sat upon the cloud swung his sickle on the earth, and the earth was reaped.

[17]And another angel came out of the temple in heaven, and he too had a sharp sickle. [18]Then another angel came out from the altar, the angel who has power over fire, and he called with a loud voice to him who had the sharp sickle, "Put in your sickle, and gather the clusters of the vine of the earth, for its grapes are ripe." [19]So the angel swung his sickle on the earth and gathered the vintage of the earth, and threw it into the great wine press of the wrath of God; [20]and the wine press was trodden outside the city, and blood flowed from the wine press, as high as a horse's bridle, for one thousand six hundred stadia.

We have been suggesting that the writer of the Book of Revelation uses symbols that are not to be restricted to only one point of reference. Each symbol is purposely designed to recall a number of reference points from within the common life and heritage of God's people. By using such symbols the traditions of the past are recalled in order to shed light on the struggles of the present.

This is nowhere more evident than in Chapters 12 and 13, which depict the struggle between the church and the worldly powers. John's churches are oppressed churches because of their witness to the Word of God and the testimony of Jesus (1:9). But such oppression should not be too surprising since throughout history God's witnesses must carry on their ministries within a fallen world. They will necessarily meet resistance even while they proclaim God's good news, for that message asks the world to turn away from its own agenda to God's, a message the world finds difficult to accept. The more forceful the proclamation, the more forceful the resistance, as Jesus well knew (cf. Matt. 23:34–37).

In Revelation 12 and 13, John depicts this resistance in terms of an epic struggle both in heaven and on earth. On earth the struggle is between a sinister dragon and a woman with child (12:1–6, 13–17). In heaven the struggle is between that same dragon and the archangel Michael, each augmented by his respective angelic hosts (12:7–12). Also on earth the dragon has his lieutenants, a beast from the sea and a beast from the earth, who carry on the oppression of God's people.

In ancient mythology it was common to portray the struggle between good and evil in terms of a great primeval battle. The Babylonian creation myth tells of the defeat of the seven-headed water monster Tiamat by Marduk, the god of light. An ancient Egyptian myth speaks of the red dragon Set who pursues the goddess Isis and is later killed by Horus her son. In Greek mythology the pregnant goddess Leto escapes from the dragon Python and gives birth to Apollo, who returns and kills the dragon. So John's portrait of the conflict between the woman with child and the red dragon with seven heads is not a new idea in the literature of the ancient world.

What is new is what John does with this imagery and the identification he makes. His task is to proclaim the good news of God's victory in Christ and to present his readers with a message of hope in their difficult situation. So he must move from cosmic generalities to the particulars of his readers' daily experience. The resources which he has at his disposal are the heritage and traditions he holds in common with his readers.

For instance, the red dragon for John is none other than "that ancient serpent, who is called the Devil and Satan, the deceiver of the whole world" (12:9). John's identification here is so powerful that on the basis of this verse alone we automatically equate Eden's serpent with Satan, even though Genesis 3 does not make that equation. John also knows that the Old Testament speaks of Zion as the mother of God's people (Isa. 54:1; cf. Gal. 4:26) and as a woman in labor whose time of child-bearing is near (Isa. 26:17; Mic. 4:10; cf. Gal. 4:19, 27). John also knows of the promises concerning the messianic child to come (Isa. 7:14; 9:6; Ps. 2:7) and of the attempts to do away with him from his birth to his cross.

John also knows of the war in heaven between Michael and Satan (cf. Jude 9) which culminated in Satan's defeat and expulsion from heaven. The archangel Michael, traditionally presented as the guardian of God's people (cf. Dan. 12:1), is victorious over Satan, traditionally presented as the adversary of God's people, accusing them of wrongdoing before God (cf. Job 1:6–11; Zech. 3:1–10). The war in heaven has been resolved (Rev. 12:7–12), and its resolution now offers certain hope for those still engaged in the struggle on earth.

Now there is no longer any place in heaven for Satan and his cohorts (Rev. 12:8), for all his accusations have been rendered useless by the cross of Christ (12:10–11). As St. Paul had written: "Who shall bring any charge against God's elect? It is God who justifies; who is to condemn? It is Christ Jesus, who died, yes, who was raised from the dead, who is at the right hand of God, who indeed intercedes for us" (Rom. 8:33–34 au. trans.).

Heaven's song of victory acknowledges that Satan's defeat was accomplished by Christ's cross (12:11), but also that because Satan sees the beginning of the end he has come down to earth "in great wrath" (12:12). The earth is the only stage remaining for the forces of evil to carry on their assault. But the apocalyptic vision is that what already is in heaven is the future for those on earth. That means that because the cross of Christ has rendered Satan's work in heaven obsolete, God's people are decisively equipped to deal with the demonic forces still desperately at work in this world.

But deal with them they must, and John knows that when Jesus' followers proclaim the good news of God's rule they are to expect Satan to "fall like lightning from heaven" (Luke 10:18). They are to *expect* resistance and fierce struggle. For the war on earth is still on! John knows of the presence of the demonic powers within his daily experience. He sees the confrontation between his churches and the Roman state as a manifestation of the struggle between God's people and the forces of evil. The woman with child is the mother of God's people (cf. Isa. 54:1), and the dragon has come "to make war on the rest of her offspring, on those who keep the commandments of God and bear testimony to Jesus" (12:17).

The dragon stands at the sea and calls his lieutenants into action (12:17, last sentence). Now John relates to the specific experiences of his readers, whose churches have been oppressed by Rome, that militant power which approached Asia Minor from the sea. The "beast rising out of the sea" (13:1) is the Roman

Empire, whose navy assailed the coasts of the eastern Mediterranean and whose armies sacked and colonized the nations. In demonic form its emperors called themselves divine and demanded their subjects to revere them as deified (13:1–4). The state had assumed the position of God, and people were deceived into thinking that its power was unlimited. But what authority the state might have is given to it and that authority will one day come to an end (13:5–7). Its conflict with the church is only temporarily permitted (13:7).

The second beast is from the earth and exercises the authority of the first beast. His duty is to see to it that the first beast is heard and worshiped (13:15) after the manner of the false prophet of Deut. 13:1 who promotes idolatry by means of miraculous signs and wonders. In John's time this image would reflect a Roman provincial governor, an imperial puppet ruler whose duty is to make sure that all those under his rule openly show their allegiance to Rome and to impose physical pressure and economic sanctions against all those who do not show such allegiance, especially against those who refuse to participate in the imperial cult (13:16–17).

This second beast has a number for its name: 666 (Rev. 13:18). Throughout the history of interpretation a great deal of speculation has taken place about the identity of this beast whose name is the number 666. A host of specific individuals has been suggested by interpreters since the second century, and usually in each case the text is forced into fitting a new conjecture. Of course, riddles are fascinating, and we know that both Greek and Jewish writers in ancient times engaged in the practice of using numbers for names and names for numbers. The letters of the alphabet were given numerical equivalents, and thus every name had a corresponding number. This practice was known among Jewish writers as *gematria,* and the rabbis loved to speculate about the meanings hidden behind the numbers found in the Scriptures.

Of all the attempts to unravel the meaning of the number 666 in Rev. 13:18, the one most commonly accepted is that 666 is the numerical equivalent of the name "Nero Caesar" in Hebrew, and that the mysterious number therefore refers to the Emperor

Nero, the infamous persecutor of Christians in Rome. Some ancient copyists of the New Testament also made this connection, but felt that they should change the number to 616 (see the *RSV* marginal note) in order to make it fit Nero's name in Latin! The problem with this theory is that John of Patmos was writing in Greek, not in Hebrew or Latin, a problem which urges us to seek another solution.

Following our principle that John's symbols are not to be exhausted by simple one-to-one equations, we should not allow the meaning of the number 666 to become sedimented with any one point of reference. Furthermore, we know the importance of the number seven for John as a symbol for completeness, for perfection. By contrast, then, the number of the second beast is "666" in order to symbolize compounded imperfection.

The first beast is Rome, and the second is Rome's lieutenant. John's immediate readers are in at least seven different locations (2:1—3:22), and in each location they must deal with the local authorities appointed by the Roman imperial power. The number 666 must be allowed the fluidity to speak to each local situation without losing its symbolic sharpness. Even though the Roman imperial might, brandished at the local level by its puppet governors, claims divine authority and seems so indestructible, the number 666 is to remind John's readers of the state's humanness, mortality, and fallibility. Neither the Roman emperor nor his lieutenants are divine, and the compound number 666 suggests they are triply imperfect, bound (as one commentator puts it) to "failure upon failure upon failure."

John's message to Christians of every time and place is that the state is not divine, and the church exists in order to distinguish between God and those who would stand in God's place and usurp God's rule. The worldly powers are not God, and no absolute allegiance is due them. The state, our state, is a human institution, far from perfect. In our language, the state is not a "ten," not a "seven," but just three miserable "sixes."

John's symbols reflect events current in the lives of his original audience, but they are also meaningful to that audience because John and his readers were also knowledgeable of the Hebrew Scriptures. By his constant use of imagery from Israel's biblical

traditions John is asserting the continuity of the Christian church
with Israel and the solidarity of God's people of the past, present,
and future. Furthermore, the use of symbol allows John's readers
of every age to apply what is said to every new situation of conflict between the church and the worldly powers. But we must
remember that John's images are images of *hope* and must not be
used as images of terror to cause even greater apprehension. For
John's main purpose is stated clearly in Rev. 13:10: "Here is a
call for the endurance and faith of the saints" (cf. also 14:12).

Therefore proper interpretation of the Book of Revelation must
begin with the situation experienced by the author and his
readers and with the traditions familiar to them. An approach to
John's writing which imposes a system alien to him and his
readers is doing justice to neither. The good news he seeks to
proclaim should not be turned into bad news by sensationalism
and fear-mongering. Nor should we give reason for the Accuser
to take up his work again, namely, to accuse us of honoring God
only for personal profit (cf. Job 1:6–11).

The Accuser, John says, has lost the battle in heaven, but the
struggle on earth is now on. This means that God's people of the
present should be every bit as disciplined as God's people of the
past. They must first of all know whom they follow—the Lamb
who was slain, Christ crucified (14:1). In contrast to those who
wear the mark of the imperial cult and engage in its excesses
(13:15–16), the people of God wear the mark of God and the
Lamb and have disciplined themselves for the struggle which
faces them (14:4–5). As we have already seen, the number
144,000 is not to be taken literally, but as a symbol for the fullness of God's people since John defines it as a multitude "which
no man could number" (7:9). In 14:4 they are as disciplined for
the present conflict as God's fighting men of old (cf. 1 Sam. 21:5).
Discipline, not asceticism, is John's point here, a discipline
which belongs to the followers of Christ crucified in whose
mouth no lie was found (14:4–5; cf. Isa. 53:9). Discipline is the
companion of endurance (14:12).

In the rest of Chapter 14 John envisions the results of the
conflict between the church and the worldly powers. He sees an
angel in the midst of heaven offering an eternal gospel to the

entire world (14:6). Along with the gospel an invitation is given to acknowledge the rule of God, the Creator of the world. In rapid succession two other angels announce the fall of the false god Rome, here called "Babylon" (14:8), and of all its worshipers (14:9–11). In contrast to 13:5–18, where those who worship the beast to avoid its wrath have temporary respite from it, the third angel offers a fierce warning of eternal doom to those who by their idolatry incur the wrath of God. In its severity this warning is a startling pronouncement, designed purposely to shock the complacent by a vivid comparison of the temporary with the eternal and also to intensify the struggle against a socially convenient apostasy.

The concluding scenes depict the final judgment, again in traditional terms. The harvester is Daniel's Son of Man in messianic attire (14:14; cf. Dan. 7:13–14; Matt. 25:31–34). In Mark 13:27 and Matt. 13:41 the Son of Man sends his angels to gather the elect and exclude the wicked. In Rev. 14:17–20 the angels also act as the vintagers, casting the grapes into "the great wine press of the wrath of God." Reminiscent of the fate of the earthly Jesus, crucified outside the city and with his blood left flowing from his side (John 19:20, 34), the grapes of judgment are pressed "outside the city" (14:20) and the splendor of the worldly powers becomes no more than a great river of blood spilled out on the earth.

The sights and sounds of 14:1–20 are grim indeed. Is there anything other than judgment and recompense portrayed in these seven word pictures of what John sees and hears? Yes, there is; for these seven word pictures (vv. 1–5, 6–7, 8, 9–13, 14–16, 17, 18–20) must not be separated from the word pictures of Chapter 13. In fact, there is an explicit connecting link between the two chapters in John's statement: "Here is a call for the endurance and faith of the saints" (13:10, 14:12). Both occurrences of this statement pose a dual admonition concerning Christian behavior toward the state: Christians are neither to capitulate to its idolatrous demands (14:9–11) nor to repay violence with violence (13:7–10). The accent is on Christian discipline (14:4), which is to be maintained under even the most oppressive of circumstances.

Such discipline is the bench mark of discipleship for those who "follow the Lamb wherever he goes" (14:4). These are the ones who remember that vengeance does not belong to them (cf. Rom. 12:19). They will remember not to assume for themselves the options that belong to God alone. Their behavior is defined by their Lord, the Lamb who was slain. That is why the seven word pictures of Chapter 14 begin with the sight of the Lamb and his followers standing on Mount Zion. John of Patmos knows Psalm 2, that even though the nations conspire and plot, God has set his king on Mount Zion, who shall rule the nations with a rod of iron (Ps. 2:1, 6, 9; cf. Rev. 11:18; 12:5). This disciplined rule has come, the Root of David is none other than the Lamb who was slain (Rev. 5:5–6), and it is he whom God has placed on his holy mountain. The Lamb rules, and neither he nor his followers need to do the work of subduing the nations. The seven visions of Mount Zion proclaim that vengeance is God's option, that it belongs to God's future, and that his people need not take it into their own hands.

10

The Seven Bowls of
God's Wrath

REV. 15:1—16:21

15 Then I saw another portent in heaven, great and wonderful, seven angels with seven plagues, which are the last, for with them the wrath of God is ended.

²And I saw what appeared to be a sea of glass mingled with fire, and those who had conquered the beast and its image and the number of its name, standing beside the sea of glass with harps of God in their hands. ³And they sing the song of Moses, the servant of God, and the song of the Lamb, saying,

"Great and wonderful are thy deeds,

O Lord God the Almighty!

Just and true are thy ways,

O King of the ages!

⁴Who shall not fear and glorify thy name, O Lord?

For thou alone art holy.

All nations shall come and worship thee,

for thy judgments have been revealed."

⁵After this I looked, and the temple of the tent of witness in heaven was opened, ⁶and out of the temple came the seven angels with the seven plagues, robed in pure bright linen, and their breasts girded with golden girdles. ⁷And one of the four living creatures gave the seven angels seven golden bowls full of the wrath of God who lives for ever and ever; ⁸and the temple was filled with smoke from the glory of God and from his power, and no one could enter the temple until the seven plagues of the seven angels were ended.

16 Then I heard a loud voice from the temple telling the seven angels, "Go and pour out on the earth the seven bowls of the wrath of God."

²So the first angel went and poured his bowl on the earth, and foul and evil sores came upon the men who bore the mark of the beast and worshiped its image.

³The second angel poured his bowl into the sea, and it became like

the blood of a dead man, and every living thing died that was in the sea.

⁴The third angel poured his bowl into the rivers and the fountains of water, and they became blood. ⁵And I heard the angel of water say,

"Just art thou in these thy judgments,

thou who art and wast, O Holy One.

⁶For men have shed the blood of saints and prophets,

and thou hast given them blood to drink.

It is their due!"

⁷And I heard the altar cry,

"Yea, Lord God the Almighty,

true and just are thy judgments!"

⁸The fourth angel poured his bowl on the sun, and it was allowed to scorch men with fire; ⁹men were scorched by the fierce heat, and they cursed the name of God who had power over these plagues, and they did not repent and give him glory.

¹⁰The fifth angel poured his bowl on the throne of the beast, and its kingdom was in darkness; men gnawed their tongues in anguish ¹¹and cursed the God of heaven for their pain and sores, and did not repent of their deeds.

¹²The sixth angel poured his bowl on the great river Eu-phra'tes, and its water was dried up, to prepare the way for the kings from the east. ¹³And I saw, issuing from the mouth of the dragon and from the mouth of the beast and from the mouth of the false prophet, three foul spirits like frogs; ¹⁴for they are demonic spirits, performing signs, who go abroad to the kings of the whole world, to assemble them for battle on the great day of God the Almighty. ¹⁵("Lo, I am coming like a thief! Blessed is he who is awake, keeping his garments that he may not go naked and be seen exposed!") ¹⁶And they assembled them at the place which is called in Hebrew Armaged'don.

¹⁷The seventh angel poured his bowl into the air, and a great voice came out of the temple, from the throne, saying, "It is done!" ¹⁸And there were flashes of lightning, loud noises, peals of thunder, and a great earthquake such as had never been since men were on the earth, so great was that earthquake. ¹⁹The great city was split into three parts, and the cities of the nations fell, and God remembered great Babylon, to make her drain the cup of the fury of his wrath. ²⁰And every island fled away, and no mountains were to be found; ²¹and great hailstones, heavy as a hundred-weight, dropped on men from heaven, till men cursed God for the plague of the hail, so fearful was that plague.

John of Patmos knows of Christians who have paid with their

lives for their resistance to Rome by their refusal to participate in the imperial cult (cf. 2:13). Efforts by the government to make Christians renounce their faith resulted in a convenient apostasy for some, but a steadfast witness to the death for others (13:15–17). Throughout history from John's day to ours oppressive governments have been wary of that Christian commitment which sees no human institution as its absolute and final authority. The martyrs are not forgotten, says John, for he hears the Spirit say: "Blessed are the dead who die in the Lord . . . for their deeds follow them" (14:13).

But these are the ones who are the conquerors mentioned in each of John's letters to the seven churches (2:7, 10–11, 17, 26; 3:5, 12, 21). In the scene that now follows (15:2), John envisions the fulfillment of God's promises to his churches and the results of their endurance. The conquerors are assembled together for the final judgment, the final outpouring of God's wrath. The victors are "those who had conquered the beast and its image and the number of its name" (15:2). Their steadfast witness through struggle, hardship, and martyrdom had brought them to share in the victory won by Christ crucified. Their song of victory is "the song of Moses, the servant of God, and the song of the Lamb":

> Great and wonderful are thy deeds,
> O Lord God the Almighty!
> Just and true are thy ways,
> O King of the ages!
> Who shall not fear and glorify thy name, O Lord?
> For thou alone art holy.
> All nations shall come and worship thee,
> for thy judgments have been revealed. (15:3–4)

This hymn echoes the song of Moses in Exod. 15:1–8, but virtually every phrase is reflected elsewhere in the Old Testament as well (Pss. 11:2; 139:14; 86:8–9; Deut. 32:4; Mal. 1:11). The song of Moses, which celebrates God's deliverance and liberation of his people, has now become the song of the Lamb, who now offers liberation to all nations.

We have noted John's constant use of imagery taken from the liturgical and literary traditions familiar to his readers. By doing this John emphasizes the continuity of the church with Israel and relates the good news of God's deliverance of his people in the past to the rigors of life in the present. In Chapter 15 the recollection of the Exodus from Egypt provides the means to speak of God's promise and judgment. For God's people the Exodus meant deliverance. But for those who chose to place their trust in their own strength, the Exodus meant judgment.

One of the four living creatures guarding God's throne now appears, distributing "seven golden bowls full of the wrath of God" (15:7). Previously, the golden bowls of Rev. 5:8 contained the incense representing the prayers of the saints. Such prayers were offered to God by those who did not trust in their own strength but who looked to him to secure their future. Now at the judgment their future is secure, and the golden bowls pour out God's answer to their oppressors (16:1–21).

One after another the bowls are emptied to inflict plagues on the earth and on the sea, on the inland waters and on the heavenly bodies, and then directly on Rome (16:2–11). The pouring out of the sixth bowl dries up the Euphrates River, opening up the eastern boundary of the Roman Empire for attack from the dreaded Parthians (16:12–16). This signals the final spectacular battle which will crumble the great Roman state, symbolized by the term "Armageddon." John's readers know the meaning behind this symbol, a play on the Hebrew term *Har Megiddo,* which means "Mount Megiddo," the stronghold where so many of history's ancient and decisive battles were fought. For them it is now a symbol of God's final deliverance of his people from their oppressors.

The contents of the final bowl are cast into the air to signal the end of the outpouring of God's wrath (16:17–21). No city on earth has been spared, but the "great city" (Rome), the center of demonic power and oppression, is ruined, along with the "Babylon" (the empire) that expands from it (16:8).

It is not easy to speak of the wrath of God. So John uses imagery available to him from his tradition, from plague to storm, earthquake to hailstone. In the Old Testament all have been vehicles for the expression of divine retribution. What purpose, we should ask, is finally served by this catastrophic panorama?

For John's churches, socially and politically powerless, the

Roman Empire seemed to be an insurmountable force. The pervasive might of the Roman state reduced every nation in its path to utter subservience. Its demands were total, reaching into the religious arena to brand as enemies of the state those who refused to engage in the official imperial religious practices. How often must the feeling have been expressed in John's churches: "Who is like the beast, and who can fight against it?" (13:4).

Therefore the recollection of the Exodus traditions became John's means of proclaiming the good news to the oppressed. John must remind his readers that they too are Exodus people. They are recipients of God's promises and therefore look toward the future he has prepared for them. As Exodus people they call no city on earth their home and give no absolute allegiance to any human institution. In contrast to their oppressors, they do not live out of their own resources, but out of the resources of the promises and future of God.

Those who live out of their own resources and seek to control their own existence on their own terms are eventually shattered. For they are not in control of their existence, and death is proof of it. But this lesson is hard to learn, and therefore John attempts to teach it in the most severe terms. Even Rome will die, and its death will be so final and so commensurate with its own vaunted cruelty that the wrath of Rome will finally be ended by the wrath of God.

11
The Fall of "Babylon"

17 Then one of the seven angels who had the seven bowls came and said to me, "Come, I will show you the judgment of the great harlot who is seated upon many waters, ²with whom the kings of the earth have committed fornication, and with the wine of whose fornication the dwellers on earth have become drunk." ³And he carried me away in the Spirit into a wilderness, and I saw a woman sitting on a scarlet beast which was full of blasphemous names, and it had seven heads and ten horns. ⁴The woman was arrayed in purple and scarlet, and bedecked with gold and jewels and pearls, holding in her hand a golden cup full of abominations and the impurities of her fornication; ⁵and on her forehead was written a name of mystery: "Babylon the great, mother of harlots and of earth's abominations." ⁶And I saw the woman, drunk with the blood of the saints and the blood of the martyrs of Jesus.

When I saw her I marveled greatly. ⁷But the angel said to me, "Why marvel? I will tell you the mystery of the woman, and of the beast with seven heads and ten horns that carries her. ⁸The beast that you saw was, and is not, and is to ascend from the bottomless pit and go to perdition; and the dwellers on earth whose names have not been written in the book of life from the foundation of the world, will marvel to behold the beast, because it was and is not and is to come. ⁹This calls for a mind with wisdom: the seven heads are seven hills on which the woman is seated; ¹⁰they are also seven kings, five of whom have fallen, one is, the other has not yet come, and when he comes he must remain only a little while. ¹¹As for the beast that was and is not, it is an eighth but it belongs to the seven, and it goes to perdition. ¹²And the ten horns that you saw are ten kings who have not yet received royal power, but they are to receive authority as kings for one hour, together with the beast. ¹³These are of one mind and give over their power and authority to the beast; ¹⁴they will make war on the Lamb, and the Lamb will conquer them, for he is Lord of lords and King of kings, and those with him are called and chosen and faithful."

¹⁵And he said to me, "The waters that you saw, where the harlot is seated, are peoples and multitudes and nations and tongues. ¹⁶And the ten horns that you saw, they and the beast will hate the harlot; they will make her desolate and naked, and devour her flesh and burn her up with fire, ¹⁷for God has put it into their hearts to carry out his purpose by being of one mind and giving over their royal power to the beast, until the words of God shall be fulfilled. ¹⁸And the woman that you saw is the great city which has dominion over the kings of the earth."

18 After this I saw another angel coming down from heaven, having great authority; and the earth was made bright with his splendor. ²And he called out with a mighty voice,

"Fallen, fallen is Babylon the great!
It has become a dwelling place of demons,
a haunt of every foul spirit,
a haunt of every foul and hateful bird;
³for all nations have drunk the wine of her impure passion,
and the kings of the earth have committed fornication with her,
and the merchants of the earth have grown rich with the wealth of her
      wantonness."

⁴Then I heard another voice from heaven saying,

"Come out of her, my people,
lest you take part in her sins,
lest you share in her plagues;
⁵for her sins are heaped high as heaven,
and God has remembered her iniquities.
⁶Render to her as she herself has rendered,
and repay her double for her deeds;
mix a double draught for her in the cup she mixed.
⁷As she glorified herself and played the wanton,
so give her a like measure of torment and mourning.
Since in her heart she says, 'A queen I sit,
I am no widow, mourning I shall never see,'
⁸so shall her plagues come in a single day,
pestilence and mourning and famine,
and she shall be burned with fire;
for mighty is the Lord God who judges her."

⁹And the kings of the earth, who committed fornication and were wanton with her, will weep and wail over her when they see the smoke of her burning; ¹⁰they will stand far off, in fear of her torment, and say,

"Alas! alas! thou great city,
thou mighty city, Babylon!
In one hour has thy judgment come."

[11]And the merchants of the earth weep and mourn for her, since no one buys their cargo any more, [12]cargo of gold, silver, jewels and pearls, fine linen, purple, silk and scarlet, all kinds of scented wood, all articles of ivory, all articles of costly wood, bronze, iron and marble, [13]cinnamon, spice, incense, myrrh, frankincense, wine, oil, fine flour and wheat, cattle and sheep, horses and chariots, and slaves, that is, human souls.

[14]"The fruit for which thy soul longed has gone from thee,
and all thy dainties and thy splendor are lost to thee, never to be found again!"

[15]The merchants of these wares, who gained wealth from her, will stand far off, in fear of her torment, weeping and mourning aloud,

[16]"Alas, alas, for the great city
that was clothed in fine linen, in purple and scarlet,
bedecked with gold, with jewels, and with pearls!
[17]In one hour all this wealth has been laid waste."

And all shipmasters and seafaring men, sailors and all whose trade is on the sea, stood far off [18]and cried out as they saw the smoke of her burning,

"What city was like the great city?"

[19]And they threw dust on their heads, as they wept and mourned, crying out,

"Alas, alas, for the great city
where all who had ships at sea grew rich by her wealth!
In one hour she has been laid waste.
[20]Rejoice over her, O heaven,
O saints and apostles and prophets,
for God has given judgment for you against her!"

[21]Then a mighty angel took up a stone like a great millstone and threw it into the sea, saying,

"So shall Babylon the great city be thrown down with violence,
and shall be found no more;
[22]and the sound of harpers and minstrels, of flute players and trumpeters,
shall be heard in thee no more;
and a craftsman of any craft
shall be found in thee no more;
and the sound of the millstone
shall be heard in thee no more;
[23]and the light of a lamp
shall shine in thee no more;
and the voice of bridegroom and bride
shall be heard in thee no more;

for thy merchants were the great men of the earth,
and all nations were deceived by thy sorcery.
[24]And in her was found the blood of prophets and of saints,
and of all who have been slain on earth."

"Babylon" is written on her forehead, on that great harlot "drunk with the blood of the saints and the blood of the martyrs of Jesus" (17:5–6). John of Patmos knows his readers' present situation as well as the biblical traditions which have nurtured their faith, their commitment to the gospel, and their liturgical practice. He can now envision their future, but only "in the Spirit" (17:3), that is, only as one of them, whose existence is shaped and conditioned by the good news of God's presence among his people.

John is initially amazed at the sight of the great harlot "Babylon." She is seated upon "many waters," which 17:15 tells us are "peoples and multitudes and nations and tongues." Because of her great might she is the object of the illicit affections of the kings of the earth, whose behavior is applauded and mimicked by their subjects (17:2). This is no common whore, this "Babylon." Her ultralavish attire is meant to attract everyone: she wears nothing but the very best (17:4). Her life style means, of course, that she must destroy those who are not attracted by her, specifically the saints and the martyrs of Jesus (17:6).

John's amazement at this macabre parasite is met with the question: "Why marvel?" (17:7). This question is directed not only to him but to his readers as well, for the following interpretation of this scene describes the very predicament in which they find themselves (17:8–18). The symbol of the great harlot "Babylon" reflects the history of John's churches and of the world in which they live. It also serves as an image of hope for those who can see past the glitter of human institutions to the future which belongs to God alone.

The harlot is a symbol for the city of Rome, the established crown of the empire and the showcase of its spirit. Her luxury, license, and power attract those who dwell on the earth, specifically those who cannot see beyond such monetary values to ask about God's future (17:8). Rome has become a false standard, a false god, one which "was and is not and is to come," in contrast to the true God "who is and who was and who is to come" (1:4, 8;

4:8). That the beast still "is to come" shows that John's description should not be limited to any one point of reference but may be applied to any human institution which devastates people by prostituting its wealth, influence, and power. In John's own time the prime example was Rome.

Further interpretation and application of his imagery, John says, must be done with great care. "This calls for a mind with wisdom" (17:9). The interpretation of John's writing must be done neither in a cavalier manner nor with a self-seeking spirit. Opportunistic sensationalism for profit reflects the values of the harlot rather than those of the exile of Patmos. The "mind with wisdom" is trained to see in John's images the good news of God without which there can be no images of hope. John's word pictures are not meant to frighten but to encourage, to call his readers to endurance (13:10), and to celebrate the gracious rule of God.

For instance, much attention has been given to two groups of kings in this chapter. Various interpreters have suggested that the seven kings of 17:10 represent the Roman emperors up to John's time, and others have said that the ten kings of 17:12 are to be applied to our own time to represent a cartel of ten European kingdoms such as the European Common Market countries. Such speculative interpretations engage in a great deal of manipulation of historical fact, and therefore they remain unconvincing. They really miss John's point here, for they attempt to limit John's message to only one or another point of reference.

Certainly for John's day the images of the beast and the harlot are symbols for Rome, both empire and city, the violent oppressor of God's people. Rome is the beast who has played god with the nations, the beast "who was and is not and is to come." But the words "is to come" mean that *Rome itself is a symbol* for any nation or human institution which assumes for itself the place of God in this world. Once again, John's symbols are tensive symbols, not to be limited to any one point of reference, and thus become vehicles for the preaching of God's Word in every time and place.

Therefore John's message is a prophetic message, a word of preaching to Christian communities, asking God's people to refuse to identify with the empty values of any system which crushes people for its personal gain. As long as history yet unfolds, the beast will always be coming, enticing people with its false values of luxury, license, and power. The "eighth" beast (17:11) will always be coming, but it really "belongs to the seven, and it goes to perdition." All such beasts—past, present, and future—belong to the seven, and the mind with wisdom will know who they are.

As is the case elsewhere in John's writing, the numbers ten and seven symbolize completeness. The seven kings represent a system which in all its fury constitutes a political, social, and moral threat to God's people. The number seven is eschatological: it signals a time of decision for God's people in which they must define their identity in terms of God's future. That future has already been secured for them by the cross of Christ, for no number of kings can overcome the Lamb "who is Lord of lords and King of kings." "Those with him," John says, "are called and chosen and faithful" (17:14).

The number ten is also eschatological and in this case represents the final end of the great harlot. Now we are ready for John's surprise. The ten kings are at first allied with the beast to war against Christ and his church (17:12–14). But at the last they turn against the great harlot herself, the city of Rome (17:16–18). John's surprise is a prophetic one: the power of evil is always self-destructive. Those who seek only luxury, license, and power will, if necessary, destroy each other in their attempts to achieve their goals. Egocentric institutions which disdain mutual respect and trust have within themselves the seeds of their own destruction. They cultivate no true allies.

So the funeral dirge begins: "Fallen, fallen is Babylon . . . (18:2–20). This dirge is an eloquent composition in which John combines elements from various Old Testament songs of lament, starting with Isa. 21:9 (cf. also Amos 5:2). This dirge records the lament of those who had been attracted by the glitter of the city and had sought in it their present and future security. Rulers, merchants, and seamen lament the sudden collapse of the power they thought so unassailable. The unexpected had happened, and quickly:

> Since in her heart she says, "A queen I sit,
> I am no widow, mourning I shall never see,"
> so shall her plagues come in a single day. (18:7–8)

Suddenly, in a single day, "in one hour" (18:10, 17, 19), that upon which so many people had placed their hopes, the highest accomplishments of secular humanity, is brought to nothing: "all thy dainties and thy splendor are lost to thee, never to be found again!" (18:14). All the achievement of the city—music, art, construction, design, festival (18:22–23)—is dissolved, for below the glossy surface was the pain and tragedy of its victims: "in her was found the blood of prophets and of saints, and of all who have been slain on earth" (18:24).

The fall of the harlot "Babylon," which God has hastened by motivating her allies to fulfill their evil designs (17:17), is nothing other than God's judgment upon her. When the hymn of victory in 19:1–3 says "Salvation and glory and power *belong* to our God" (italics added), we are meant to know that God has his rights too, and among those rights belongs God's judgment of the oppressor and the salvation of his own people. But this right of God is not quickly exercised, for even at the very last when "Babylon" is fallen and her evil core is laid bare, there is still a voice from heaven issuing that gracious invitation:

> Come out of her, my people,
> lest you take part in her sins,
> lest you share in her plagues. (18:4)

Readers of today may not immediately see the gospel of God in this invitation nor the historical allusions behind it. The dominant motif in these two chapters is the fall of the great harlot who has committed illicit relations with the nations of the earth. The beginning of the dirge repeats this motif (18:2–3), and we might think that the words of the invitation in 18:4 simply extend the language of this motif. But with the words "Come out of her, my people," John's original readers would recall God's redemptive invitations of the past. They would remember the times in the past when God had not left his people alone and had gone to retrieve them from hopeless situations. With the words "lest you take part in her sins," they would remember God's gracious invitation to Lot and his family to leave Sodom (Gen. 19:12), and with the words "lest you share in her plagues," they would remember God's gracious invitation to come out of Egypt (Exod. 3:7–22). John has already prepared them for these recollections by his earlier identification of Rome with Sodom and Egypt (Rev. 11:8).

That John's symbols have their roots in the church's Old Testament heritage is nowhere clearer than in the use of the code word "Babylon" for the city of Rome (cf. also 1 Pet. 5:13). No more sinister enemy of God's people could be envisioned than that ancient Mesopotamian empire which destroyed Israel's Temple, brought her Davidic kingship to an end, and transported her people away from the land of promise. The capital city of that empire was Babylon, known for its luxury and moral corruption. The great prophets of the Old Testament, such as Isaiah and Jeremiah, had to contend with the sense of hopelessness brought about by the ruthless oppression this empire inflicted on God's people. For them "Egypt" and "Sodom" were code words of promise, images of hope that the God who had redeemed his people in the past would not forget them in the present (Isa. 43:3, 16–17; Jer. 50:40). John of Patmos knows that ancient Babylon, like ancient Egypt and ancient Sodom, were but preludes to God's gracious deliverance of his people. John believes this also of Rome and gives this hope expression by means of the symbol "Babylon."

Therefore this elegantly composed funeral dirge in Rev. 18:2–20 begins with words taken directly from Isaiah (21:9), "Fallen, fallen is Babylon." Throughout the dirge the images employed constantly reflect Old Testament material, mainly from the prophetic writings. Rev. 18:4 is modeled after Isa. 13:21–22, where the fallen Babylon will be inhabited only by wild beasts and howling creatures. That Babylon's sins are "heaped high as heaven" (18:5) recalls Jer. 51:9, and the concept of double recompense (18:6) has precedents in Isa. 40:1, Jer. 16:18 and 17:18. The harlot's words in 18:7 are patterned after Babylon's words in Isa. 47:8, "I am, and there is no one besides me; I shall not sit as a widow or know the loss of children." Such allusions to the biblical prophetic writings continue throughout the rest of the dirge over the Babylon that has fallen.

It is clear that John composed this dirge purposely to recall the message of hope proclaimed by the biblical prophets. Their ministry of offering a word of encouragement to God's people in a time of oppression is now John's ministry; their message is now his message. The emphasis is on hope, for this dirge is not a petulant malediction against a human institution, but a striking word picture of the mortality of every human institution and of the folly of allowing our lives to be determined by what is mortal and human. The emphasis is on hope, for in the very midst of the dirge is God's gracious and redemptive invitation addressed to those of folly and hopelessness, "Come out of her, my people, lest you take part in her sins, lest you share in her plagues" (18:4).

12
The Final Victory

REV. 19:1—20:15

19 After this I heard what seemed to be the mighty voice of a great multitude in heaven, crying,

"Hallelujah! Salvation and glory and power belong to our God,
²for his judgments are true and just;
he has judged the great harlot who corrupted the earth with her fornication,
and he has avenged on her the blood of his servants."
³Once more they cried,
"Hallelujah! The smoke from her goes up for ever and ever."
⁴And the twenty-four elders and the four living creatures fell down and worshiped God who is seated on the throne, saying, "Amen. Hallelujah!" ⁵And from the throne came a voice crying,
"Praise our God, all you his servants,
you who fear him, small and great."
⁶Then I heard what seemed to be the voice of a great multitude, like the sound of many waters and like the sound of mighty thunderpeals, crying,
"Hallelujah! For the Lord our God the Almighty reigns.
⁷Let us rejoice and exult and give him the glory,
for the marriage of the Lamb has come,
and his Bride has made herself ready;
⁸it was granted her to be clothed with fine linen, bright and pure"—
for the fine linen is the righteous deeds of the saints.

⁹And the angel said to me, "Write this: Blessed are those who are invited to the marriage supper of the Lamb." And he said to me, "These are true words of God." ¹⁰Then I fell down at his feet to worship him, but he said to me, "You must not do that! I am a fellow servant with you and your brethren who hold the testimony of Jesus. Worship God." For the testimony of Jesus is the spirit of prophecy.

¹¹Then I saw heaven opened, and behold, a white horse! He who sat upon it is called Faithful and True, and in righteousness he judges and

makes war. [12]His eyes are like a flame of fire, and on his head are many diadems; and he has a name inscribed which no one knows but himself. [13]He is clad in a robe dipped in blood, and the name by which he is called is The Word of God. [14]And the armies of heaven, arrayed in fine linen, white and pure, followed him on white horses. [15]From his mouth issues a sharp sword with which to smite the nations, and he will rule them with a rod of iron; he will tread the wine press of the fury of the wrath of God the Almighty. [16]On his robe and on his thigh he has a name inscribed, King of kings and Lord of lords.

[17]Then I saw an angel standing in the sun, and with a loud voice he called to all the birds that fly in midheaven, "Come, gather for the great supper of God, [18]to eat the flesh of kings, the flesh of captains, the flesh of mighty men, the flesh of horses and their riders, and the flesh of all men, both free and slave, both small and great." [19]And I saw the beast and the kings of the earth with their armies gathered to make war against him who sits upon the horse and against his army. [20]And the beast was captured, and with it the false prophet who in its presence had worked the signs by which he deceived those who had received the mark of the beast and those who worshiped its image. These two were thrown alive into the lake of fire that burns with brimstone. [21]And the rest were slain by the sword of him who sits upon the horse, the sword that issues from his mouth; and all the birds were gorged with their flesh.

20 Then I saw an angel coming down from heaven, holding in his hand the key of the bottomless pit and a great chain. [2]And he seized the dragon, that ancient serpent, who is the Devil and Satan, and bound him for a thousand years, [3]and threw him into the pit, and shut it and sealed it over him, that he should deceive the nations no more, till the thousand years were ended. After that he must be loosed for a little while.

[4]Then I saw thrones, and seated on them were those to whom judgment was committed. Also I saw the souls of those who had been beheaded for their testimony to Jesus and for the word of God, and who had not worshiped the beast or its image and had not received its mark on their foreheads or their hands. They came to life, and reigned with Christ a thousand years. [5]The rest of the dead did not come to life until the thousand years were ended. This is the first resurrection. [6]Blessed and holy is he who shares in the first resurrection! Over such the second death has no power, but they shall be priests of God and of Christ, and they shall reign with him a thousand years.

[7]And when the thousand years are ended, Satan will be loosed from his prison [8]and will come out to deceive the nations which are at the four corners of the earth, that is, Gog and Magog, to gather them for battle;

their number is like the sand of the sea. [9]And they marched up over the broad earth and surrounded the camp of the saints and the beloved city; but fire came down from heaven and consumed them, [10]and the devil who had deceived them was thrown into the lake of fire and brimstone where the beast and the false prophet were, and they will be tormented day and night for ever and ever.

[11]Then I saw a great white throne and him who sat upon it; from his presence earth and sky fled away, and no place was found for them. [12]And I saw the dead, great and small, standing before the throne, and books were opened. Also another book was opened, which is the book of life. And the dead were judged by what was written in the books, by what they had done. [13]And the sea gave up the dead in it, Death and Hades gave up the dead in them, and all were judged by what they had done. [14]Then Death and Hades were thrown into the lake of fire. This is the second death, the lake of fire; [15]and if any one's name was not found written in the book of life, he was thrown into the lake of fire.

When the hymn of victory in 19:1 declares that "Salvation and glory and power *belong* to our God" (italics added), we are meant to know that God has his rights also, and among them is his judgment of those who attempt to usurp his rule. Rome's emperors had demanded worship and reverence as deities and had assumed for themselves titles such as *dominus et deus*, "Lord and God," and *soter*, "Savior." But the prophetic vision is that the final victory will not belong to them or to the empire they have built. The final victory belongs to God, and God himself hastens the fall of "Babylon" by giving her the freedom to carry out her corruption to its inevitable self-destructive conclusion (17:17). Among the rights of God alone is the salvation of his people, which he constantly offers until the very last moment (18:4).

Salvation belongs to God. That is his proper work, and no one takes it from him or offers it in his stead. A number of images in Chapters 19 and 20 reinforce this theme. The fourth of seven beatitudes in the Book of Revelation proclaims: "Blessed are those who are invited to the marriage supper of the Lamb" (19:9). This beatitude reflects two traditional images used among Christians to portray God's eschatological salvation: the great wedding feast (cf. Matt. 22:3–14) and the church as the Bride of Christ (cf. 2 Cor. 11:2). The final victory of God's people means the joyous celebration of a new beginning, of a new life together with their Lord:

> Hallelujah! For the Lord our God the Almighty reigns.
> Let us rejoice and exult and give him the glory,
> for the marriage of the Lamb has come,
> and his Bride has made herself ready. (Rev. 19:6–7)

This hymn of triumph then makes the important point that the church is equipped by God for salvation, when it says concerning the Bride: "*it was granted her* to be clothed with fine linen, bright and pure" (italics added). John adds the explanatory remark, "for the fine linen is the righteous deeds of the saints" (19:8; cf. Phil. 3:8–21). The statement in Rev. 19:9 that "these are true words of God" is to be applied to the entire section (17:1— 19:9) regarding the fall of "Babylon."

The warrior on the white horse in 19:11–21 is a word picture of Christ himself. As one who carries out God's salvation and judgment he is called "Faithful and True" (19:11). As one whose weapon is his word (19:13; cf. 1:16; 2:16), he is called the "Word of God." As one who stands in contrast to the frightful but feeble earthly powers, he is "Kings of kings and Lord of lords" (19:16). This portrait of Christ is not to suggest only the exalted Christ who will return in glory but is also meant to include the earthly Jesus in his own prophetic ministry, in which the evil powers had already tasted defeat. In John's theology the victor is none other than the crucified; the triumphant ruler of the nations is none other than the Lamb who was slain. The mark of his conquest is on his robe: it is dipped in blood—his own (8:13; cf. 7:14; 12:11).

The conqueror and his forces are now posed for the final victory. That it is final is indicated by the summons to all the birds of the air to participate in the destruction of the enemy. Again, in order to stress the finality of this conflict, John uses imagery known to his readers from the Old Testament (Ezek. 39:17–20). There is also a progression in the conquest over the forces of evil: the fall of the harlot "Babylon" is followed by the fall of the beast and the false prophet (19:17–21)—first the city of Rome, then the empire, then its local human manifestation. With his lieutenants now out of commission, Satan himself is the next on the list of adversaries to be dealt with, and after him Death and Hades (20:1–15).

How does this frightful battle scene square with John's admonition to his readers to avoid warfare? In 13:10 he urged his readers not to use violent means to resist the authorities who persecute them. If they engage in such violent action, they are to expect violent retribution. But now John depicts the final overthrow of the church's enemies in a most militant way: the conqueror on the white horse, Christ himself, will lead the armies of heaven in furious battle toward the final victory (19:11–21). Is John being inconsistent?

No he is not. He is careful to state that his readers themselves do not participate as combatants in that furious battle. Although the forces of evil (19:19) gather to wage war against Christ and his armies, not even the heavenly armies of the conqueror are involved in the eventual triumph. That triumph is won by Christ alone: he smites the nations with his Word, he treads the wine press of the fury of God's wrath (19:15), and "the rest were slain by the sword of him who sits upon the horse, the sword that issues from his mouth" (19:21). This word picture describes the means by which the final victory is accomplished: it is won by Christ alone, by his Word alone, without the militant help of his followers. His followers are even to forget about the spoils: the spoils are for the birds (19:17–18, 21).

It is in this context that we must understand the much disputed chapter on the millennium (20:1–15). In this chapter, and only here in the entire New Testament, we hear of a period of one thousand years in which Satan is bound and Christ reigns with those of his followers who have suffered martyrdom. It is this number which is expressed by the term "millennium," a combination of the two Latin words *mille* (thousand) and *annus* (year). The effect of this section on John's immediate readers is that they are not to expect the final victory over Satan, Death, and Hades to come immediately, even within their own lifetimes (20:5). Like all the other numbers John has been using, the one thousand years are to be taken symbolically as the time of God's remembrance and reward for those whose lives have been cut short because of their witness to Christ. It is a long time, God's time, and no one plans it for him. No one knows when it begins and when it ends.

So the millennium is not for everyone, not even for every Christian. It is a special time for Christ and his martyrs (20:4). During this time Christian living and dying continues on earth with all human living and dying until God's time is fulfilled (20:5). That means that while Satan is bound, Death is still active, with all its consequences (21:8). Corruption and injustice take place in this world without there having to be a personal devil on the loose. And when the end of God's long time has come, the final victory will include the end of Satan, Death, and Hades and all their followers in the "second death" (20:15; 21:8). They will be judged by what they have done (20:13).

So death is not the last word in the Christian vocabulary. Nor is it a new word. John's vision is that God remembers those who have died for their witness to Christ, and their lives are restored to them in his own way and in his own time, never to be taken from them again (20:6). Christians who have not been martyred are also not forgotten. For when in God's own way and in his own time they stand before his judgment, they need not fear the second death either, for their names are already etched in God's memory, inscribed in his book of life.

13

The New Heaven and
the New Earth

REV. 21:1—22:5

21 Then I saw a new heaven and a new earth; for the first heaven and the first earth had passed away, and the sea was no more. ²And I saw the holy city, new Jerusalem, coming down out of heaven from God, prepared as a bride adorned for her husband; ³and I heard a great voice from the throne saying, "Behold, the dwelling of God is with men. He will dwell with them, and they shall be his people, and God himself will be with them; ⁴he will wipe away every tear from their eyes, and death shall be no more, neither shall there be mourning nor crying nor pain any more, for the former things have passed away."

⁵And he who sat upon the throne said, "Behold, I make all things new." Also he said, "Write this, for these words are trustworthy and true." ⁶And he said to me, "It is done! I am the Alpha and the Omega, the beginning and the end. To the thirsty I will give water without price from the fountain of the water of life. ⁷He who conquers shall have this heritage, and I will be his God and he shall be my son. ⁸But as for the cowardly, the faithless, the polluted, as for murderers, fornicators, sorcerers, idolaters, and all liars, their lot shall be in the lake that burns with fire and brimstone, which is the second death."

⁹Then came one of the seven angels who had the seven bowls full of the seven last plagues, and spoke to me, saying, "Come, I will show you the Bride, the wife of the Lamb." ¹⁰And in the Spirit he carried me away to a great, high mountain, and showed me the holy city Jerusalem coming down out of heaven from God, ¹¹having the glory of God, its radiance like a most rare jewel, like a jasper, clear as crystal. ¹²It had a great, high wall, with twelve gates, and at the gates twelve angels, and on the gates the names of the twelve tribes of the sons of Israel were inscribed; ¹³on the east three gates, on the north three gates, on the south three gates, and on the west three gates. ¹⁴And the wall of the city had twelve foundations, and on them the twelve names of the twelve apostles of the Lamb.

[15]And he who talked to me had a measuring rod of gold to measure the city and its gates and walls. [16]The city lies foursquare, its length the same as its breadth; and he measured the city with his rod, twelve thousand stadia; its length and breadth and height are equal. [17]He also measured its wall, a hundred and forty-four cubits by a man's measure, that is, an angel's. [18]The wall was built of jasper, while the city was pure gold, clear as glass. [19]The foundations of the wall of the city were adorned with every jewel; the first was jasper, the second sapphire, the third agate, the fourth emerald, [10]the fifth onyx, the sixth carnelian, the seventh chrysolite, the eighth beryl, the ninth topaz, the tenth chrysoprase, the eleventh jacinth, the twelfth amethyst. [21]And the twelve gates were twelve pearls, each of the gates made of a single pearl, and the street of the city was pure gold, transparent as glass.

[22]And I saw no temple in the city, for its temple is the Lord God the Almighty and the Lamb. [23]And the city has no need of sun or moon to shine upon it, for the glory of God is its light, and its lamp is the Lamb. [24]By its light shall the nations walk; and the kings of the earth shall bring their glory into it, [25]and its gates shall never be shut by day—and there shall be no night there; [26]they shall bring into it the glory and the honor of the nations. [27]But nothing unclean shall enter it, nor any one who practices abomination or falsehood, but only those who are written in the Lamb's book of life.

22 Then he showed me the river of the water of life, bright as crystal, flowing from the throne of God and of the Lamb [2]through the middle of the street of the city; also, on either side of the river, the tree of life with its twelve kinds of fruit, yielding its fruit each month; and the leaves of the tree were for the healing of the nations. [3]There shall no more be anything accursed, but the throne of God and of the Lamb shall be in it, and his servants shall worship him; [4]they shall see his face, and his name shall be on their foreheads. [5]And night shall be no more; they need no light of lamp or sun, for the Lord God will be their light, and they shall reign for ever and ever.

Nowhere in the Book of Revelation does John of Patmos leave his readers without hope. His vivid descriptions of corruption and injustice and his stern denunciations of the oppressor are never left to stand by themselves. His criticisms of his churches in Chapters 2 and 3 are always accompanied by a promise, namely, that in spite of all appearances, those who remain faithful to Christ do indeed have a future. His pictures of destruction, from the four horsemen to the seven trumpets to the seven bowls, always include the word of God's victory after the evil forces have had their day. And even at the last, when the fall of the oppressor is assured, God's voice can be heard above the tumult, calling to him those who will still listen (18:4).

Now at the end of this writing John of Patmos offers his crowning image of hope, his vision of a new heaven and a new earth (21:1—22:5). John is not the first to use such imagery, for the apocalyptic writings of Ethiopic Enoch, Esdras, and Baruch already spoke of the renewal of the creation at the end of the ages. In the Christian tradition before him Paul had spoken of the time when the creation would be liberated from its bondage to decay (Rom. 8:19–22), and after him Hebrews 8 and 2 Peter 3 spoke of the dissolution of the old order and the emergence of the new. John knows God's promise, "Behold, I make all things new" (21:5), and he now sets out to describe that promised new world.

But the last thing John wants to offer is a pie-in-the-sky portrait of a dreamland utopia far removed from the human scene. Everything he has said so far has had direct contact with his immediate readers' current situation, and his expert use of symbol has allowed future readers to relate his message to their own commitment to the gospel in every age. How does John's picture of God's new world relate to the struggles of his readers, past and present?

First, the centerpiece in a world created anew by God is a new city, the new Jerusalem. It is a "holy city," that is, a city set apart for God's use in the world. It stands in contrast to the corrupt city of Chapters 17 and 18, as "a bride adorned for her husband" (21:2) stands in contrast to the harlot "Babylon" (the city of Rome), "with whom the kings of the earth have committed fornication" (17:2).

This new city is not a remote oasis beyond the clouds, but it comes down from heaven to the world of human beings, for it is among human beings that God wishes to dwell (21:2–3). Earlier St. Paul had spoken of "the Jerusalem above" as the mother of the liberated community of God's people (Gal. 4:26). Now John concretizes this freedom: in contrast to the old city which lived off the pain and tragedy of its victims (18:24), God's new city will provide healing for the nations (21:4; 22:2). The new Jerusalem is the manifestation of "God with us" as expressed in the covenant promise: "I will be your God and you shall be my people" (21:3, cf. Lev. 26:12; 21:7, cf. 2 Sam. 7:14). In Rev. 21:3, a particular Greek word is used to express God's "tabernacling" among his people, the same word as is used in John 1:14: "The Word became flesh and dwelt ('tabernacled') among us."

The careful description of this new city in 21:9—22:9 employs imagery from Ezekiel 40—48 as well as terms of measurement found in historical descriptions of ancient cities, including Jerusalem, Babylon, and Rome. Again, the new Jerusalem stands in contrast to its old counterparts and adversaries and therefore offers a living alternative to John's readers. For example, the sea was a means of economic (18:17–19) and military (13:1) expansion for Rome, and therefore a source of exploitation and dread for other peoples. In the new city there is no sea (21:1), for its evil inhabitants have been dealt with and pose no further threat (20:13–14). In the new city instead of the destructive sea, there is "the river of the water of life . . . flowing from the throne of God and of the Lamb" (22:1).

In contrast to Ezekiel, where attention is focused on the description of the Temple, the new Jerusalem envisioned by John has no temple at all, "for its temple is the Lord God the Almighty and the Lamb" (21:22). In the new city there is no official religious institution and therefore also no separation between church and state. There is also no separation between this city and the nations: the latter have free access to this city, for its gates are always open (21:25). There is no need for security, for the dangers of dark night are no more. The light which is now available to the nations is "the glory of God . . . and its lamp is the Lamb" (21:23).

Neither is this a one-way transaction: as the nations walk in the light of this city, they bring to it their own glory and honor (22:24–26). In God's new city there are no barriers placed before the foreigners: those who come to the city are one with those who dwell there (21:27).

In most cities the city wall encompasses the city proper. This is not so in the new Jerusalem (21:15–17). The city itself is cube-shaped and measures "twelve thousand stadia" (about fifteen hundred miles) on each side, far out of proportion to the city wall, which measures only 144 cubits (about 216 feet). This means that the wall is not to serve as protection around the city but as a nucleus within it. It has twelve gates named after the twelve tribes of Israel and twelve foundations named after the twelve apostles. One cannot help but recall the words of Eph. 2:19–20: "You are no longer strangers and sojourners, but you are fellow citizens with the saints and members of the household of God, built upon the foundation of the apostles and prophets, Christ Jesus himself being the cornerstone."

The wall of this nucleus is painstakingly described in 21:18–21. It is made of the most precious gems, signifying its inestimable value as a life center to the city surrounding it. For within it is the throne of God and the Lamb, from which flows the healing waters of the river of life (22:1). The tree of life, withheld from humanity since the fall, now offers its fruit without ceasing (22:2). The face of God, withheld since the fall, will now be seen by everyone (22:4).

From this precious nucleus, from God and the Lamb, flows the life of the city of the nations. Therefore John's emphasis on transparency: the city was made of gold, clear and transparent as glass (21:18, 21), and the first jewel in each foundation stone was jasper, a transparent gem. This means that in all that is done in the city, in all its daily activity, what remains visible is the source of its life, God and the Lamb. The new city reflects the center of its being, God and the victorious Christ who was crucified, for all things now are new. There is healing among the nations: no more corruption (21:27), no more racism (22:3), no more dangers of the night (22:5).

It all seems so far from our world. Or does it? Are not Christians now called to a living transparency, to reflect in their lives the God who has acted in Christ crucified and risen? John thought so and said that in their faithful struggle Christians will bear the name of God's new city, the new Jerusalem, and God's own name, and Christ's own name (3:12). St. Paul thought so too, for he said that if anyone is in Christ, there is a new creation, a new world, a new heaven, a new earth (cf. 2 Cor. 5:17 in the New English Bible translation).

14

The Epilogue

⁶And he said to me, "These words are trustworthy and true. And the Lord, the God of the spirits of the prophets, has sent his angel to show his servants what must soon take place. ⁷And behold, I am coming soon."

Blessed is he who keeps the words of the prophecy of this book.

⁸I John am he who heard and saw these things. And when I heard and saw them, I fell down to worship at the feet of the angel who showed them to me; ⁹but he said to me, "You must not do that! I am a fellow servant with you and your brethren the prophets, and with those who keep the words of this book. Worship God."

¹⁰And he said to me, "Do not seal up the words of the prophecy of this book, for the time is near. ¹¹Let the evildoer still do evil, and the filthy still be filthy, and the righteous still do right, and the holy still be holy."

¹²"Behold, I am coming soon, bringing my recompense, to repay every one for what he has done. ¹³I am the Alpha and the Omega, the first and the last, the beginning and the end."

¹⁴Blessed are those who wash their robes, that they may have the right to the tree of life and that they may enter the city by the gates. ¹⁵Outside are the dogs and sorcerers and fornicators and murderers and idolaters, and every one who loves and practices falsehood.

¹⁶"I Jesus have sent my angel to you with this testimony for the churches. I am the root and the offspring of David, the bright morning star."

¹⁷The Spirit and the Bride say, "Come." And let him who hears say, "Come." And let him who is thirsty come, let him who desires take the water of life without price.

¹⁸I warn every one who hears the words of the prophecy of this book: if any one adds to them, God will add to him the plagues described in this book, ¹⁹and if any one takes away from the words of the book of this prophecy, God will take away his share in the tree of life and in the holy city, which are described in this book.

²⁰He who testifies to these things says, "Surely I am coming soon."
Amen. Come, Lord Jesus!

²¹The grace of the Lord Jesus be with all the saints. Amen.

The Book of Revelation concludes with an epilogue which is
made up of a series of statements fit rather loosely together. In
the prologue (1:1–8), we were able to detect a certain progression
based on literary interests and liturgical order. Such a progression is difficult to discover in the epilogue, and sometimes we
must assume who the speaker actually is (22:6 = the angel of
21:9? But 21:7 = Jesus. 21:10 = God? But 21:12 = Jesus.). However, there are two main interests in this concluding section:
(1) the truthfulness, authority, and inviolability of what has previously been written; and (2) the nearness of Christ's coming.

One can also see that a relationship has purposely been drawn
between the epilogue and the prologue in terms of verbal similarities and subject matter. For instance, there is the restatement
of the theme of reception, that God is the source of the message
that John has shared with his audience, mediated to him from
Jesus through an angelic messenger (22:6, 16; cf. 1:1). There is
also the reference to the entire writing as "the words of
prophecy" (22:7, 10, 18–19; cf. 1:3), to be read in the churches
(22:18; cf. 1:3, 11). Those who keep the words of this prophecy
are blessed (22:7; cf. 1:3). There are the Alpha and Omega theme
(22:13; cf. 1:8), beatitudes (22:7, 14; cf. 1:3), a word of grace
(22:21; cf. 1:4), and the announcement of Christ's coming soon
(22:6–7, 12, 20; cf. 1:1, 7). Such purposely drawn similarities with
the prologue are meant to provide a structural balance as well as
a greater unity to the writing as a whole.

We should therefore expect the epilogue to restate themes
heard elsewhere in the book other than those in the prologue.
For instance, the warning to John is repeated that he should not
confuse the mediating messenger with God, the source of the
message—a warning that the church in every time and place
needs to hear (22:8–9; cf. 19:10). Other repeated themes include:
the access of God's people to the tree of life in the new holy city
(22:14, 19; cf. 22:2); a list of vices (22:15; cf. 21:8); the testimony
to the churches as delivered by the messenger sent by Jesus
(22:16; cf. 2:1—3:22).

The warning in 22:18–19 against adding to or taking away from the words of this book is often misunderstood as a reference to the entire Bible. This misunderstanding occurs because these words from the Book of Revelation stand also at the end of the New Testament canon. Precisely because of misunderstandings like this we have urged that our interpretation of Revelation begin first of all with John of Patmos and his intentions, and for John the New Testament had not yet been compiled; indeed, he was still in the process of writing what later became part of the New Testament. So in his warning in 22:18–19 he is speaking of what *he* has written. The words "this book" and "this prophecy" in Rev. 22:18–19 refer to the Book of Revelation which John of Patmos is now completing. What does he mean by issuing such a warning?

First, John may be well aware of the growing editorial practice in the church of not only copying but also revising and adjusting the words of earlier Christian writings which continued to be used throughout the churches. Examples of such writings would be collections of the teachings of Jesus and the letters of Paul. John could be pleading for a responsible accuracy in such work. But it is even more likely that John's warning is that of a general appeal to "every one who hears" (22:18) to allow John's prophecy to speak in all its sharpness and challenge. John's stern warning is similar to Paul's own warning against those who pervert the gospel (Gal. 1:6–9) and who thereby turn it into something it is not intended to be. A perverted gospel is no gospel at all, and John's message of hope should not be turned into a message of despair.

In order to make sure that we have heard this message of hope John includes in the epilogue the final two of the seven beatitudes in the Book of Revelation. These seven beatitudes are:

Blessed is he who reads aloud the words of the prophecy, and blessed are those who hear, and who keep what is written therein. (1:3).

Blessed are the dead who die in the Lord henceforth. (14:13)

Blessed is he who is awake, keeping his garments that he may not go naked and be exposed! (16:15)

Blessed are those who are invited to the marriage supper of the Lamb. (19:9)

Blessed and holy is he who shares in the first resurrection. (20:6)

Blessed is he who keeps the words of the prophecy of this book. (22:7)

Blessed are those who wash their robes, that they may have the right to the tree of life and that they may enter the city by the gates. (22:14)

The function of the beatitudes is the reversal of the values of the world outside God's city. God's blessing rests upon those who assemble with his people who are gathered around his Word (1:3; 22:7), who have remained faithful to their Lord throughout their lives (14:13), who are alert and prepared for their Lord in every opportunity (16:15), who value his invitation (19:9; 22:14), and who live in terms of his future (20:6). The world outside God's city has different values (22:15). Yet to any who thirst for the waters of life, the invitation remains open (22:17; cf. 18:4). This invitation finally becomes mutual: God invites the one who hears, and the one who hears is thereby enabled to invite God in return (22:17). Those first invited by God are now enabled to say "Come, Lord Jesus!" without fear of his presence, with joyful anticipation of what their Lord's presence really means. The presence of Christ means fellowship and celebration. Therefore the church celebrates the presence of its Lord whenever Christians gather together, and at the eucharistic meal the ancient *maranatha* (Aramaic for "Come, Lord Jesus," 22:20; cf. 1 Cor. 16:22) is the church's affirmation of readiness to live each day in the presence of Christ. As we learned in the letters to the seven churches, Christian anticipation of Christ's coming has implications for Christian living *now*. When Christians pray "Come, Lord Jesus," we are reminded to ask ourselves whether in our church and in our lives the presence of Jesus Christ is seen and heard, celebrated and proclaimed, envisioned and lived—and not in the future, but *now*.

The last word to be heard in John's writing is a word of grace, both the literary and the liturgical conclusion of Christian address (22:21). The Book of Revelation began as a letter and concludes with the benediction commonly used in Christian correspondence (cf. 1 Cor. 16:23; 2 Cor. 13:14; Gal. 6:18; Phil. 4:23; etc.). But John also began with recollections from the community's worship, "in the Spirit on the Lord's day" (1:10), and now he closes with the eucharistic *maranatha* and the benediction which will be heard by his churches as his writing is read aloud: "The grace of the Lord Jesus be with all the saints." John's last literary action is at the same time a liturgical action, a benediction. And his last word invites all his readers and all his hearers to join in the "Amen."

Conclusion

The genius of John's writing is that it challenges its readers to be as creative as John has been. That does not mean that John would allow them to run helter-skelter with his writing in every interpretive direction possible. His symbols are not meant to be used in such a way that his intentions for them are forgotten. So the first step in interpreting the Book of Revelation is to ask about John's own intentions, what his symbols are to reflect to his own original audience, and what message he offered which that audience needed to hear. Then we shall be able to see how that message projects itself beyond its original historical setting to us in our time, and how John's symbols can become reflectors to inform the life of the church in every age. In this concluding chapter we shall make some suggestions concerning this interpretive approach, namely, how John's message addresses the modern church.

History and Society in John's Apocalypse

John of Patmos chose to write in apocalyptic form, but his modifications of that form were in themselves statements to his original readers concerning his intentions. One of these modifications is a *literary-structural* one: his "apocalypse" is also a letter and a word of prophecy, that is, of preaching. This combination of apocalypse, letter, and expository sermon shows that John's writing is uniquely designed for use in the Christian community as both personal communication and public proclamation. But John has offered some *theological* modifications which are by no means subtle and which we should now briefly review.

Apocalyptic writers, for example, typically foresee the end of

history and the destruction of the natural world order before the
victorious reign of God and his Messiah can begin. John of Patmos, however, stresses that it is within this world and its history
that God's victory has begun. The ancient mythological struggle
between the people of God and the forces of evil is decided not
in some other world beyond history but in this world and within
its history. The victory has been won by the cross of Christ and
continues to be won by his followers through the witness they
bear in this world (Rev. 12:10–11). The conflict between the
ancient Accuser and the hosts of heaven is finally resolved by the
crucified and the gospel preached in his name.

Therefore a direct line is drawn in Rev. 15:3–4 between the
Exodus and the cross of Christ: the victory song of Moses is now
the victory song of the Lamb who was slain. Far from urging his
readers to look past their historical existence to a transcendent
future in heaven, John repeatedly calls for their critical involvement within the process of history: the "conqueror" is the Christian who endures in the present struggle after the example of
Christ crucified (2:7, 11, 17, 26; 3:5, 12, 21). A specific style of
Christian endurance is urged within present world conflict, and
that style is not escapism from it (13:10; 14:12). The new heaven
and the new earth is not a remote heavenly oasis to which John's
readers will be taken but is featured by the new Jerusalem, God's
own new city, which "comes down" to the world of human beings among whom God wishes to dwell (21:1–3).

In the description of this new city of God (21:1—22:5) a clear
contrast is drawn with the old cities of this world, principally
ancient Rome, whose values and life style are criticized by the
contrast. We must consider what a seemingly impossible task this
must have been for a politically powerless (3:8), socially suspect
(2:9) group of small, scattered Christian churches openly to confront the pervasive might of the Roman Empire, to refuse to
capitulate to imperial demands for intellectual and spiritual allegiance, and to insist that no human institution can play God in
this world.

Perhaps that is the most challenging word John has to say to
the Christians of today. John of Patmos invites us all to take a
critical look at our relationship to the political, social, and eco-

nomic institutions with which we are involved and to ask whether we are willing to offer an effective Christian witness *now*. Are we committed to institutions which destroy people and the work of God's creation? If so, the Book of Revelation calls us to rethink that commitment. It tells us that we have a prior commitment to the God who by the cross of Christ has freed us from the forces of destruction. If we now see those forces at work in our institutions, then we are committed to a witness which can transform these institutions and move them away from destructive toward constructive consequences and goals.

No human institution is to play God in this world. That is a message which is to be applied also to the church. Twice in the Book of Revelation, John is told not to confuse the messenger of God with God, the source of the message (19:10; 22:8–9). Every church, our church, must ask whether it is providing an effective witness to the presence of Christ or whether its Lord has actually become secondary to its own self-interests. No human institution is to play God in this world, not even the church. John's words, just as the victor's sword, are not single-edged: the letters to the seven churches insist that the Word of God is promise and challenge for both world and church (2:12). By listening carefully to John's words we shall see that they are not a message from the distant past about the coming future, but a message which works its way into our present and confronts us with our own responsibilities in our world now.

A further common feature of traditional apocalyptic writings is a dualism in which the struggles of the present are seen in terms of the universal battle between the forces of good and evil, heaven and hell, light and darkness. This feature is present in John's writing also, but with a thoroughgoing Christian modification: the battle has already been won by Christ crucified. Therefore there is no need to fear the oppressor nor any need to show contempt toward those influenced by the oppressor. Instead of contempt there is understanding for those who stood in awe of the glitter of the empire (18:9–24). Instead of contempt the invitation is still extended, up to the very last: "Come out of her, my people" (18:4).

The nations have been deceived by the old corrupt city

(18:23). Now from God's new city flow the waters of healing—for the nations (22:1–2). This means that God's new city is not reserved only for the small enclave of the righteous, nor is it reserved only for those who in their devotion to God withdraw in contempt for the rest of society. The new city of God is for those who know themselves to be in need of healing, for the thirsty. In God's new city there is no contempt (22:3), but rather his continuous invitation: "To the thirsty I will give water without price from the fountain of the water of life" (21:6).

Reading Revelation in an Apocalyptic Age

It is a rare day when one opens the newspaper and fails to find reports of new political kidnappings, of hostages held for ransom, of assassinations, renewed terrorist activities, and general escalation toward nuclear war. Oppressive governments carry on wholesale summary executions; human beings become "displaced" and refugees have increasingly fewer places to flee for refuge; arms production increases while world hunger and disease continue unabated. These are grim years, apocalyptic years in an apocalyptic century.

Will the world make it past the present decade? Some say it will not. The anxiety produced by current events has led to a demand to know what the future will bring and often to look to the Book of Revelation to provide the answers. But using Revelation to chart the course of modern history usually produces even more anxiety and tends to obscure the intentions of John of Patmos and the good news he wanted to proclaim. It is hoped that by now we have learned to appreciate Revelation best by keeping in mind its original historical context. So we begin first with John, the instrument of God's good news, to see how that news was good to its original readers.

At the beginning of the book John's message is set within the context of Christian worship (1:10). John begins there for various reasons. It is in the congregational worship setting where John can best identify with his readers, as both he and they experience persecution by the secular government under which they must live their daily lives (1:9). It is there that they confess their faith together (1:2), hear God's Word together (1:3), receive God's blessing together (1:4). Each day they face the powers of death and hell, but in their congregational worship assemblies they hear the good news of him who has the keys of death and hell (1:18). They assemble to hear the good news of Christ's presence among them, and in their worship together their eyes are fixed on him (1:12–16).

In this context we can understand what John means when he calls his writing a word of "prophecy" (1:3). It is a word of preaching, of proclamation to sisters and brothers in Christ. It is a word of comfort and encouragement, "a call for the endurance and faith of the saints" (13:10; 14:12). Far from predicting what things will be like twenty centuries later, John wishes to address his own churches with a message that speaks to their own difficult situation. In the worship setting he is encouraged to remember his own ordination and that he has been called to proclaim the presence of Christ even now (1:17). The word that he is given to proclaim is not his own word (2:1, 8, 12, 18; 3:1, 7, 14), and therefore he cannot withhold it. It is a prophetic word, a word from God to his people.

By no means does John speak in vague generalities. In Chapters 2 and 3 he addresses seven congregations whose inner life and public witness he knows well. Even in their time of oppression the Word of the gospel comes to them with its expectations: they are to remain living examples of love and courage; their witness must remain clear and unique; they must continue to offer authentic life and healing to their communities. John writes to seven churches, but by choosing the number seven, a symbol for completeness, he is addressing all Christian churches in every time and place. What is true for one is true for all. This means that the symbols that John chooses have a certain transparency: even though they are specific, they are not exhausted by any one point of reference.

This is especially the case with John's depiction of the oppressor of his churches, namely, the Roman government. Rome and its forces are depicted with various symbols, the beasts from the sea and the earth and the whore of Babylon (Chapters 13—18). John and his churches have heard of the claims of "Rome Eternal" and of the "divine Caesars," and they know the feeling of

helplessness in the face of such an overwhelming power. But
they also know that only God is eternal. God alone is the one
"who is and who was and who is to come," "Alpha and Omega,"
the beginning and the end (1:8). They are to keep this in mind
whenever they hear the claims of any human institution, for
Christians are called in every time and place to distinguish between the human and the divine, and to help others to do so also.

This does not mean that Christians display a contemptuous
death wish for all that is human. Their Lord became human and
died for humans. The churches are now his instruments for car-
ing for what is human. They are to witness to his presence in the
world and to be examples of love, truth, justice, and peace. They
are in the world and they participate in its humanness, but they
are God's instruments for healing among the nations. Therefore
there is no running into the wilderness to await Armageddon, no
whiling away the hours in feverish expectation and paranoid
speculation, no religious flights into the spiritual stratosphere, no
flights from the cities, the laboratories, the classrooms, the
sickbeds—no flights at all. For God's new city comes down to
earth (21:2) and offers healing to the nations (22:2).

There is a season in the church year called "Advent," the four
weeks prior to Christmas in which the church considers the
meaning of the past, present, and future coming of Christ. It is in
the context of the Advent season that we can best understand the
words "Behold, I am coming soon" (22:7; 12:20). This is Alpha
and Omega speaking, not just Omega. This is the one who was
and is, not just the one who is to come. The "I" who is coming
soon is also the one who has come and is come. Christians believe in the presence of Christ now among his churches (1:12),
and therefore they cannot speak of his absence at all. He comes
to them constantly—in word and sacrament, wherever two or
three are gathered together in his name. His final coming is up to
him, for *he* is Omega, not we. With his presence now Christians
have much to celebrate, much witness to bear, much ministry to
perform—as they always have, as they do now, and as they will
in the future.

Will the world make it past the present decade? We do not
know. We do not have to know. For John of Patmos, the purpose

of Christian prophecy is not to predict God's future but to bear witness to Christ now (19:10). Christ is present in his Word, and without that prophetic Word people are left to pursue their own selfish aims. With that prophetic Word people are called to care for one another, to encourage one another, to provide for one another. The prophetic Word of God's good news is that the future belongs to God, and therefore the future of his people is secure.

John's prophecy ends as it began, in the context of Christian worship. When his churches prayed the ancient *maranatha,* "Come, Lord Jesus" (22:20), they acknowledged that they do not live their lives alone out of their own resources, but that all that they do is conditioned by their commitment to Christ crucified and risen. So from eucharistic meal to family meal Christians of today join John of Patmos and his churches to celebrate Christ's presence among them: "Come, Emmanuel! Come, Lord Jesus!"

Appendix A

APOCALYPTIC LITERATURE

At various points in our study we have mentioned other Jewish and Christian apocalyptic writings with which the Book of Revelation can be compared, most of which are not to be found in the Bible. The reader may desire to know when these writings first appeared and where they might be found for further reading. We shall therefore list the major apocalyptic writings with brief comments about their dates of origin.

For the complete English translations of Jewish apocalypses other than the Old Testament book of Daniel, the reader may consult the two-volume work by R. H. Charles, *Apocrypha and Pseudepigrapha of the Old Testament* (Oxford: At the Clarendon Press, 1913). For the complete English translations of Christian apocalypses other than the New Testament Book of Revelation, the reader may consult the two-volume work by E. Hennecke and W. Schneemelcher, *New Testament Apocrypha* (Philadelphia: Westminster Press, 1963 and 1965). Both works have helpful introductory information on each individual writing, although some conclusions (especially in the collection of Charles) are now somewhat outdated.

We shall not list all the examples of apocalyptic literature which have come down to us, but rather some major representative writings of this category, Jewish and Christian.

1. Jewish Apocalypses
    a. Daniel. The Old Testament book of Daniel is dated by most scholars between the years 167–164 B.C. The strictly apocalyptic material in the book is to be found in Chapters 7—12.

b. 1 Enoch. This writing is also called "Ethiopic Enoch" because it exists in complete form only in Ethiopic translation. Written originally in either Hebrew or Aramaic, this work is actually a collection of smaller writings of pre-Christian origin, some of which may be as early as the fourth century B.C. and others as late as the beginning of the first century A.D. First Enoch is to be distinguished from a 2 Enoch or "Slavonic Enoch," which is another collection of segments which appeared at various stages in the first century A.D. Both writings appear to have been quoted by the Christian author of the Epistle of Barnabas at the end of the first century.

c. 4 Ezra. This writing is the second of two books in the Old Testament Apocrypha attributed to Ezra. The name "4 Ezra" comes from the time before the Apocrypha were gathered into a separate category apart from the other thirty-nine Old Testament writings. Before this separation the Old Testament books of Ezra and Nehemiah were known as 1 and 2 Ezra, with the two apocryphal books known as 3 and 4 Ezra. After the separation of the apocryphal writings into their own category, which happened at the time of the Reformation, the two books of Ezra also came to be known as 1 and 2 *Esdras*. Therefore 4 Ezra and 2 Esdras, confusing as it is, are one and the same book. The book comes from the period of the late first century A.D. after the Roman conquest of Jerusalem in A.D. 70.

d. 2 Baruch. This writing is to be dated at the same time as 4 Ezra, at the end of the first century A.D. It is called "2 Baruch" to distinguish it from the (first) book of Baruch, which is among the Old Testament Apocrypha.

2. Christian Apocalypses
   a. The Apocalypse of Peter. Written toward the end of the second century, its contents include expansions of Jesus' teaching about the end of time in Mark 13 (and parallels in Matthew 24 and Luke 21). It was written in Greek and is not to be confused with the later Coptic and Arabic Apocalypses of Peter.

b. The Ascension of Isaiah. Written at the end of the first century or the beginning of the second, this Christian work combines a story about the martyrdom of the prophet Isaiah with a description of Isaiah's ascension (Chapters 6–11) through the seven heavens where he is shown various mysteries pertaining to Christ and the church. Chapter 4 contains the oldest account of St. Peter's martyrdom in Rome.

c. The Sibylline Oracles. This is a collection of books written in imitation of the oracle-giving of the Greek prophetesses, the Sibyls. Most of the books are commonly dated in the second century, but the first two were originally composed as early as the first century by a Jewish author and expanded in the second century by a Christian editor. The oracles present a systematic review of the past history of the world and the coming future, including the general resurrection of the dead, personal immortality, and cosmic transformation.

d. The Apocalypse of Paul. This work is later than the writings previously mentioned here and is dated no earlier than the middle of the third century A.D. It presents itself as the revelation Paul received, as mentioned in 2 Cor. 12:2–4. This work indicates that apocalyptic writing continued to be a popular form of expression long after the first century.

Of course, other writings could be named also, but a comprehensive review of all the apocalyptic literature that has come down to us is beyond the scope of our study. Let this list suffice as a brief overview of examples of this literature, otherwise only generally alluded to in the course of our study.

Appendix B

FOR FURTHER READING

Where do we go from here? That is a question which needs to be asked after every introductory study. The following is a list of suggestions for further study of the Book of Revelation.

1. Introductory Works

Hanson, Paul D. "Apocalypse, Genre." "Apocalypticism," *Interpreter's Dictionary of the Bible*, Supplementary Volume (Nashville: Abingdon Press, 1976), pp. 27–34. Hanson distinguishes between "apocalypse" as a type of literature, "apocalyptic eschatology" as a particular religious perspective, and "apocalypticism" as a sociological ideology.

Pilch, J. J. *What Are They Saying About the Book of Revelation?* (New York: Paulist Press, 1978). Pilch offers a very readable review of present-day scholarship on Revelation.

Schmithals, Walter. *The Apocalyptic Movement: Introduction and Interpretation* (Nashville: Abingdon Press, 1975). This is a discussion of the literature and theology of Jewish and Christian apocalypticism.

2. Popular Commentaries

Ellul, Jacques. *Apocalypse: The Book of Revelation* (New York: Seabury Press, 1977). This is not a verse-by-verse commentary, but an attempt to grasp the theological movement of Revelation as a whole, always relating the message to the modern world.

Fiorenza, Elisabeth Schüssler. *Invitation to the Book of Reve-*

lation (Garden City: Doubleday Image Books, 1981). A commentary with a general readership in mind. Good for group discussion purposes.

3. Detailed Commentaries

Caird, G. B. *The Revelation of St. John the Divine,* Harper's New Testament Commentaries (New York: Harper & Row, 1966). An easily understood, verse-by-verse commentary.

Mounce, Robert H. *The Book of Revelation,* The New International Commentary on the New Testament (Grand Rapids: Wm. B. Eerdmans, 1977). For a scholarly audience, the verse-by-verse commentary presents a wealth of information concerning scholarly discussion on each problem and offers a balanced, though generally conservative, perspective.